Alexander the Great: A Very Short Introduction

VERY SHORT INTRODUCTIONS are for anyone wanting a stimulating and accessible way in to a new subject. They are written by experts, and have been translated into more than 40 different languages.

The Series began in 1995, and now covers a wide variety of topics in every discipline. The VSI library now contains over 350 volumes—a Very Short Introduction to everything from Psychology and Philosophy of Science to American History and Relativity—and continues to grow in every subject area.

Very Short Introductions available now:

**Available soon:**

For more information visit our website
www.oup.com/vsi/

Hugh Bowden

# ALEXANDER THE GREAT

## A Very Short Introduction

OXFORD
UNIVERSITY PRESS

# OXFORD
UNIVERSITY PRESS

Great Clarendon Street, Oxford, OX2 6DP,
United Kingdom

Oxford University Press is a department of the University of Oxford.
It furthers the University's objective of excellence in research, scholarship,
and education by publishing worldwide. Oxford is a registered trade mark of
Oxford University Press in the UK and in certain other countries

Published in the United States of America by Oxford University Press
198 Madison Avenue, New York, NY 10016, United States of America

British Library Cataloguing in Publication Data
Data available

Library of Congress Control Number: 2014931678

ISBN 978-0-19-870615-1

Printed and bound by
CPI Group (UK) Ltd, Croydon, CR0 4YY

*For Isabel and Clare*

# Acknowledgements

The inspiration for writing this book came from many years teaching a course on Alexander the Great to students in the Department of Classics in King's College London. I have learned a great deal from them, and I hope that they will appreciate the results. The course was usually co-taught with Dr Lindsay Allen, who opened my eyes to the importance of the Near Eastern material. I am particularly grateful to her, and to all my colleagues at King's. I have learned much also from colleagues with whom I have discussed Alexander at conferences and lectures across the world, including Sulochana Asirvatham, Elizabeth Baynham, Philip Bosman, Brian Bosworth, Peter Green, Waldemar Heckel, Tim Howe, Robin Lane Fox, Sabine Müller, Daniel Ogden, Frances Pownall, Joseph Roisman, Andrew Stewart, Richard Stoneman, Pat Wheatley, Josef Wiesehöfer, and Ian Worthington. Most of the writing was done while I was Margot Tytus Fellow in the Department of Classics at the University of Cincinnati: I am grateful for the wonderful generosity and hospitality of the faculty and staff there. Thanks are due to all those at Oxford University Press involved in the production of the book, including Carol Carnegie, Kay Clement, Carrie Hickman, Andrea Keegan, Emma Ma, Joy Mellor, and Subramaniam Vengatakrishnan. Finally, as always, I want to acknowledge the support of my family—my wife Jill and my daughters, to whom this book is dedicated.

# Contents

# List of illustrations

# Timeline of Alexander's life

## A note on dates

The surviving ancient narratives about Alexander do not always give precise chronological information. Events mentioned in Babylonian astronomical diaries can be dated precisely, but for events mentioned by Greek writers, even if they give precise dates, we can only provide approximate equivalences, because Greek and Macedonian calendars did not work with a 365-day year, and thus were often out of alignment with the solar calendar. Therefore most dates here are given by season, but even these must be considered approximate.

| | | |
|---|---|---|
| 356 | Summer | Birth of Alexander |
| 338 | Summer | Battle of Chaeronea |
| 337 | Spring | 'League of Corinth' created |
| 336 | Spring | Macedonian forces under Parmenion cross into Asia |
| 336 | | Assassination of Philip II: Alexander becomes king |
| 335 | Spring | Alexander campaigns in Thrace and Illyria |
| | Autumn | Sack of Thebes |

| | | | |
|---|---|---|---|
| 334 | Spring | Alexander crosses the Hellespont into Asia | |
| | | Alexander at Troy | |
| | | Battle of the Granicus | |
| | Summer | Alexander liberates Greek cities of Asia | |
| | Autumn | Alexander in Caria | |
| | Winter | Alexander in Lycia | |
| 333 | Spring | Alexander at Gordium | |
| | Summer | Alexander in Cilicia | |
| | Autumn | Battle of Issus | |
| | Winter | Siege of Tyre begins | |
| 332 | Summer | Siege of Tyre ends | |
| | Autumn | Siege of Gaza | |
| | Winter | Alexander enters Egypt | |
| 331 | Spring | Alexander visits the oracle of Amun in Siwa | |
| | | Alexander marches from Egypt to Tyre, then to the Euphrates | |
| | 1 October | Battle of Gaugamela | |
| | 20 October | Alexander enters Babylon | |
| | Winter | Alexander enters Susa | |
| 330 | Spring | Alexander enters Persepolis | |
| | | Alexander burns the palace of Persepolis | |
| | Summer | Death of Darius III; Bessus declares himself king (as Artaxerxes V) | |
| | Autumn | Trial and execution of Philotas and execution of Parmenion | |
| 329 | Spring | Alexander enters Bactria and Sogdiana | |
| | | Capture of Bessus | |
| | Autumn | Alexander crosses the Jaxartes River | |
| 328 | Autumn | Killing of Cleitus | |

| | | |
|---|---|---|
| 327 | Spring | Alexander captures the Sogdian Rock |
| | | Alexander marries Rhoxane |
| | | 'Pages Plot'; arrest of Callisthenes |
| | Summer | Alexander enters the Hindu Kush |
| 326 | Spring | Alexander captures the Rock of Aornus |
| | | Alexander crosses the Indus River |
| | | Alexander defeats Porus on the Hydaspes River |
| | Summer | Alexander reaches the Hyphasis River, then returns to the Indus |
| | Winter | Alexander is wounded fighting the Malli |
| 325 | Summer | Alexander reaches the Indus Delta |
| | Autumn | Alexander marches through Gedrosia |
| | Winter | Alexander returns to Pasargadae and Persepolis |
| 324 | Spring | Alexander reaches Susa and rewards soldiers for the Indian campaign |
| | | Alexander marries Stateira and Parysatis, as part of a mass wedding |
| | | Alexander punishes satraps who abused their positions in his absence |
| | Summer | Alexander reorganizes his army |
| | | Alexander decrees the return of Greek exiles to their cities |
| | Autumn | Death of Hephaestion |
| | Winter | Alexander campaigns against the Cossaeans |
| 323 | Spring | Alexander enters Babylon |
| | June 11 | Death of Alexander |

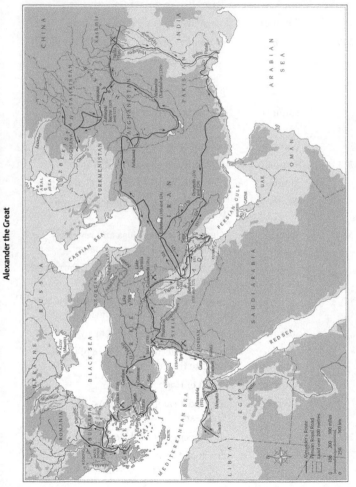

**Map 1. Map of Alexander's campaigns**

# Introduction

On the mezzanine level of the National Archaeological Museum in Naples is a large mosaic depicting a battle (Figure 1). Although the left-hand part of it is quite damaged, it is easy to pick out the figure of Alexander the Great, bare-headed, on his horse, looking intently at Darius III, who rises above the rest of the mass of horses and men, standing in his chariot, looking and pointing at Alexander in obvious alarm. Just behind Darius his charioteer is whipping his team of horses to drive him away from the imminent danger: Alexander has just run his lance through the last Persian horseman to stand between him and his opponent. Behind, the skyline is bristling with Macedonian pikes, while the foreground is littered with abandoned weapons and fallen Persians. A Macedonian victory is inevitable. The mosaic, which is nearly 6 metres long and over 3 metres high, was created not long before 100 BCE, for the owner of the House of the Faun in Pompeii. This was one of the largest private houses in Pompeii, built probably by a leading Italian aristocrat, and the mosaic occupied a prominent place in it, covering the floor of an *exedra*, a reception area where every important visitor to the house would see it. The owner clearly considered that he benefited from association with the image of Alexander as heroic warrior king.

Alexander the Great was born in 356, and was king of Macedon from 336 to his death in 323. As king, he led an army into the

1. The Alexander Mosaic: an Italian view of Alexander the Great, based on an earlier Greek painting, and depicting his victory at the battle of Issus, or possibly Gaugamela

territory of the Achaemenid Persian empire, and took control of a territory that consisted of what is now Modern Greece, parts of Bulgaria, Turkey, Syria, Lebanon, Israel, Palestine, Jordan, Egypt, parts of Libya, Iraq, Iran, Afghanistan, parts of Uzbekistan and Tajikistan, and most of Pakistan. The story of his campaigns was constantly retold after his death and, almost uniquely among figures from classical antiquity, he was never absent from the popular imagination across Europe and the Near East, from his lifetime until the present day. It is not surprising then that Alexander should be the subject for a piece of Italian art made some two centuries after his death. But asking some questions about the mosaic will help us to think about Alexander himself, and what we really know about him. It will turn out that Alexander is a rather more enigmatic figure than he might appear.

So what is the Alexander Mosaic, and what does it represent? It is agreed that the mosaic itself was created sometime between 120 and 100, but many scholars have argued that it was a copy of an older Greek painting, probably painted in the late 4th century, not long after the event it portrays. Attempts have been made to attribute it to a named painter, with candidates including Philoxenos of Eretria, or a woman, Helen of Alexandria. Since no certainly ascribed work by any ancient painter survives, these attributions do not get us very far. There is debate about which battle the mosaic depicts: Alexander encountered Darius twice, at the battles of Issus (333) and Gaugamela (331). Most scholars prefer Issus, but there is again no possibility of certainty. Does it in any case depict the battle accurately, or is it largely a work of artistic imagination? And what of other figures in the picture? Who is the man in the distinctive white helmet with a gold wreath just to the left of Alexander himself? Is it his personal seer, Aristander of Telmessus, or perhaps one of his bodyguards, Ptolemy, who went on to become ruler of Egypt, and may possibly have commissioned the picture on which the mosaic is based? Some people have rightly raised the question of whether it is appropriate to treat the Alexander Mosaic simply as a 'Roman

3

copy' of a Greek original, and then treat the image as if it actually were a 4th century painting. What we have is an Italian artwork, and attention should be paid to the context of its creation in Pompeii in the late 2nd century: what did it mean to the man who commissioned it, and the artists who worked on it, and indeed to the men and women who saw it when they visited the House of the Faun? These questions are no easier to answer, but at least they are questions about the work of art we have, rather than its imagined original.

Such concerns may not seem crucial when we are dealing with an artistic representation of one moment in Alexander's life. But very similar questions can be asked about the literary evidence for Alexander's career. The surviving narratives of Alexander's life and deeds date from between 30 BCE and the 2nd or 3rd centuries CE. The earliest surviving account that has come down to us is the work of Diodorus of Sicily, who wrote a massive *Library of History* in 40 books, starting in mythical times and extending to the death of Julius Caesar. Much of the work has been lost, but most of the seventeenth book, which is devoted to Alexander, has survived. Then there is the *History of Alexander the Great of Macedon* by the Roman, Quintus Curtius Rufus, who wrote in the reign either of Claudius or Vespasian, in the 1st century CE, and a biography of Alexander written by the Greek Plutarch of Chaeronea sometime around 100, and an account of his campaigns by another Greek, Arrian of Nicomedia, a friend of the emperor Hadrian, writing in the first third of the 2nd century. Finally, at some point after this, another Roman writer, Justin, produced an epitome, that is an abbreviated version, of the *Philippic Histories* of Diodorus' contemporary, Pompeius Trogus, which included an account of the reign of Alexander. These writers are collectively referred to as the Alexander historians. Their narratives are clearly directly or indirectly based on accounts written in the decades following Alexander's death, in several cases by men who accompanied Alexander on his campaigns, but how faithfully the authors of the surviving texts transmitted what they read is not certain. It is clear that, to a greater or lesser extent, the surviving accounts have been shaped to appeal to a contemporary readership, that is to say a readership of Greeks and Romans living in a world governed by powerful emperors, for whom Alexander might serve as a model for how to rule, or how not to rule. Fundamentally, the Alexander of the narrative sources is a Roman Alexander.

Like the Alexander Mosaic, the narrative accounts of Alexander's career probably preserve much material that goes back to Alexander's time, but what we have is in part fragmentary, and as a whole transmitted through the work of people from later centuries, who have transformed the material to suit new techniques and changed tastes. Finding effective ways to interpret these narratives is a challenge that faces anyone trying to tell the story of Alexander's life and campaigns. In many places the Alexander historians provide conflicting versions of the same set of events—and indeed Arrian notes that sometimes even eye-witness sources disagree with each other. On the other hand, when the same story appears in several different narratives, we cannot be certain that it is true: some stories about Alexander were invented in or soon after his lifetime, for example that he met, and slept with, the mythical Queen of the Amazons, and these stories rapidly became part of the narrative tradition. Some stories about him became so popular that no author could afford to ignore them, even if they could not be found in the accounts of the earliest writers. Despite decades of research into the sources of the Alexander historians (sometimes referred to by the German word *Quellenforschung*) we still have no reliable way of determining how much, if any, of their accounts can be trusted.

We can, however, make some progress in determining what is more or less likely to have happened by trying to build up a fuller picture of the world around Alexander, and to do this we need to look at more material evidence. In a case in the Ancient Iran gallery of the British Museum is displayed a small fragment of greyish terracotta, 4–5 cm wide and 6 cm high, inscribed with

5

neat lines of cuneiform script (Figure 2). The fragment, written in Akkadian, is part of a Babylonian astronomical diary referring to the second month of the fourteenth year of the king's reign. Towards the bottom of the fragment the following can be read: 'On the 29th [day] the king died; clouds [ . . . ] the sky'. The date corresponds to 11 June 323, and the king was Alexander the Great. This small piece of clay is a near-contemporary piece of evidence for Alexander, but this is a very different Alexander from the one on the mosaic. We have texts of astronomical diaries like this covering the period from 652 to 60 BCE. Every night men would stand on the roof of the king's palace in Babylon to observe the heavens. When it was not cloudy, they would note down the position of the planets, and any other unusual phenomena (comets, eclipses, and so on). These observations would then be

2. A fragment of an astronomical diary from Babylon recording events in the second month of year fourteen of Alexander's reign, including the king's death

recorded in diaries, and after each month's observations there would be a report on the prices of staple goods in the market, and notes of any significant events that had occurred. The aim of these observations was to establish the attitude of the gods to the city and to the king in particular: if signs in the sky indicated that the king faced danger, steps could be taken to protect him. Alexander first entered Babylon on 20 October 331, and was almost certainly recognized as its new king at that time. He returned to the city in the Spring of 323, and died there a few months later. While he was in the neighbourhood of Babylon, the whole system of the Babylonian scholar-priests was focused on his well-being, and his actions were recorded in royal chronicles and other kinds of text. There was a Babylonian Alexander as well as a Roman one.

A further vision of Alexander can be found on coins issued in the period after his death by the men who took control of the various parts of his empire. Alexander himself did not issue coins with his portrait on at all: instead he followed an earlier Macedonian practice of putting the head of Heracles on his silver issues. His successors started the practice of issuing coins with his portrait on them, which indicates that, like the owner of the House of the Faun somewhat later, they saw an association with Alexander as being advantageous to them. But the Alexander of these coins had unusual attributes. Some coin portraits show Alexander with ram's horns around his ears (Figure 3). These horns were the symbol of the Egyptian god Amun, whose temples in Thebes Alexander restored, and whose oracular shrine at Siwa in the Libyan desert he visited in the Spring of 331. According to the Alexander historians, it was after this visit that Alexander began to claim that he was the son of Amun (or of Zeus, with whom Amun was identified), and these claims were a major cause of resentment from Alexander's soldiers, and his companions; and most modern scholars have accepted this idea. But the coins indicate that some of these same companions actually chose to advertise the relationship between Alexander and Amun themselves. It is possible that their attitude to Alexander's claims changed after his

**3. Alexander depicted with ram's horns, the symbol of the Egyptian god Amun, on a silver coin of one of his successors, Lysimachus**

death, but it is also possible that the coins, which date from the late 4th century, are telling a truer story than the narratives written hundreds of years later.

There are other images of Alexander that can help us build up a better picture of how he was seen by his contemporaries or near-contemporaries. Greek cities inscribed and erected copies of decrees he made about them; Athenian orators referred to his activities in their surviving speeches. His name and his image, in pharaonic style, were carved into the walls of the temples of Upper Egypt where restoration work was done in his name. Still other contemporary documents and artefacts can help us get a fuller picture of the world in which he operated, even when they do not mention him by name.

While it does not ignore the narratives provided by the Alexander historians, this *Very Short Introduction* to Alexander the Great attempts to give greater weight than has been customary to these contemporary documents, and to indicate what we do not know, as well as what we do. Although it is broadly chronological in its structure, it is not intended to provide a straightforward narrative of Alexander's life and his campaigns. As it happens, Plutarch's *Life of Alexander*, which is the only one of the ancient narratives to provide an account, not necessarily to be trusted, of Alexander's childhood as well as his actions as king, is about the length of a *Very Short Introduction*, and would make a suitable companion to this one. However, the timeline provided here, along with the map showing Alexander's progress (Map 1), should be enough to prevent the reader getting lost. The next chapter, 'Before Alexander', will give a brief history of the Achaemenid Persian empire and the kingdom of Macedon, before they came into conflict, while the last chapter will explore the way Alexander's memory has continued to haunt the world in the millennia following his death. In between, we will examine Alexander in his own world: not just Greece and Macedonia, but the whole complex web of places that made up the ancient Near East.

# Chapter 1
# Before Alexander

In around 513 BCE the Persian king Darius I (522–486) built a great bridge across the Bosporus, the narrow strait that links the Black Sea with the Sea of Marmara, and led an army from Asia into Europe. Darius himself crossed back into Asia the following year, but he left his commander Megabazus with the task of subduing the territories on the north coast of the Aegean Sea. Among the local rulers who gave earth and water to the Persians as a sign of their submission was Amyntas, a Macedonian. He was rewarded with the position of *satrap* of Macedonia, that is governor of what was now a province of the Achaemenid Persian empire, and he married his daughter Gygaea to a leading Persian called Bubares. When Amyntas died in around 495, he was succeeded by his son Alexander I, who remained a loyal subject of Darius and his son and successor Xerxes. In this way the Persians themselves established in power the family that would, 180 years later, bring down their own empire. Alexander I's great-great-great-grandson was Alexander III, generally known as Alexander the Great.

## The rise of Achaemenid Persia

The Achaemenid empire was the creation of Cyrus the Great (*c*.559–530), who began as king of Anshan. This title indicated his rule over the ancient kingdom of Elam in what is now southwest Iran. Soon after coming to power around 559, Cyrus started a campaign of conquest, defeating his northern neighbours the Medes (550), and then spreading his power east over the Iranian plateau, and west into Anatolia, where he defeated Croesus, king of Lydia (546), and as a result extended his empire to the shores of the Aegean Sea. He then turned his attention to Babylon in Mesopotamia, at the time the most powerful city in the Near East. Under their kings Nabopolassar (626–605) and Nebuchadnezzar (604–562), the Babylonians had overthrown the Neo-Assyrian empire, which had dominated Mesopotamia and the territory to its west (that is roughly modern Iraq, Syria, Lebanon, Israel, Palestine, and Jordan), for several centuries, and made an empire for themselves. In 539 Cyrus defeated a Babylonian army at Opis, on the Tigris River, and entered Babylon, where he deposed its king, Nabonidus (556–539), installing his own son Cambyses in his place. Cyrus' campaigns continued until his death, and Cambyses (530–522) expanded the empire further, with the annexation of Cyprus and then Egypt (525).

Cambyses died on his journey back from Egypt—it is unclear from what cause—and was apparently succeeded by his brother Bardiya (522). At this point, however, there was a coup, and Darius, a Persian noble perhaps distantly related to the family of Cyrus, made himself king. He was able to put down a number of revolts, and, once established in power, continued his predecessors' policy of expansion. In the east he extended the empire as far as the Indus River in modern Pakistan, and he also increased his territory in north Africa, annexing the area of Cyrenaica (in modern Libya). He crossed the Bosporus in order to campaign against the Scythians on the shores of the Black Sea (c.513), and although this was not successful, it left Darius in control of the lands between the north Aegean coast and the Danube, consisting of Thrace and, as we have seen, Macedonia.

## Ruling the empire

To maintain hold over so large and disparate an empire required effective organization. Central to the Achaemenid system was the person of the king himself. Persian royal inscriptions emphasize the identity of the king, his right to rule, and the fact that he has the support of the chief of the gods, Ahura Mazda. He is shown in sculptured scenes in royal palaces and elsewhere seated on his throne or standing, always larger than other people, and often with the flying disk that represented Ahura Mazda above him. Achaemenid iconography adopted features of Assyrian royal representations, for example showing the king hunting lions. These images were used on seals, and so were disseminated across the empire. Once Darius had entered Europe he and his successors started to mint coins in the Lydian capital Sardis, gold 'Darics' depicting the king as a warrior armed with bow and spear, which circulated in the Aegean area.

The empire had several royal capitals: Cyrus ruled from Ecbatana in Media, Babylon, and Pasargadae, created by him in Fars; Darius built himself a palace at Susa in Elam, and another new creation, Persepolis, not far from Pasargadae. The king and his court moved slowly from capital to capital during the year, partly in response to the climate (Ecbatana on the Iranian plateau was cooler in the summer months, while Babylon and Susa were more appropriate for the winters). The royal progress took the form of a grand procession, and the king spent much of the time living in tents rather than stone or brick buildings, as he also did when on military campaign. This nomadic style was distinctively Persian, in contrast to the urban focus of his Mesopotamian predecessors. Palaces in the capitals were also places where royal power could be displayed. The ruins of Persepolis, the palace built by Darius I and extended by his successor Xerxes (486–465) are the most spectacular surviving example. Sculptured friezes on the outside of its *apadana* (audience hall) depict the king's subjects from across the empire bringing him tribute. Each group is distinguished by their clothes and hairstyles, and the gifts they are carrying. Non-perishable items, including large quantities of gold and silver, were stored in the palaces (when he captured them, Alexander found in the storerooms precious metals worth, at a minimum, the equivalent of 2,500 tonnes of silver, according to the ancient authors). As well as receiving tribute kings gave gifts to their courtiers and subjects, although the reciprocity was not even. For example when the king dined, he oversaw at the same time the feeding of his family, his retainers and courtiers, and his guard, through the institution of 'the king's table'.

The provinces of the empire were ruled by satraps appointed by the king. These were often leading Persian nobles, but as we have seen, local dynasts like Amyntas of Macedon could be put in charge. They were connected to the king and to each other through marriages, and although some satrapies would be passed down through families, personal bonds to the king remained important. Satraps were required to collect taxes and tribute for the king as well for themselves, and to raise troops when called upon for the king's military campaigns. These men (and occasionally women) had palaces in their own satrapal capitals, where they kept their own courts. Some had summer palaces and lodges built within great hunting parks called 'paradises' where they could imitate the king by hunting lions and other animals. Monuments like the tomb of Mausolus, satrap of Caria (377–353), built at Halicarnassus (modern Bodrum), which was included in the list of the Seven Wonders of the World, demonstrate the ambition of local dynasts who served as satraps. The courts and palaces of the western satrapies were frequently visited by leading men from beyond the edge of the empire, and acted as models for royal courts in the Aegean area, in particular in Thrace and Macedonia. For the king to oversee the activities of the satraps required good communications, and the road system of the Achaemenid empire was admired in antiquity. It made possible the rapid movement of couriers ('neither snow, nor rain, nor the heat of the sun, nor the night prevents them from completing their appointed course at greatest speed' said Herodotus, writing in the 5th century), the progresses of the royal court, and the movement of armies—both those of the king and those of invaders.

## Persia and the Greeks

The Achaemenid empire reached its greatest extent, if only briefly, under Darius' son and successor Xerxes, who conquered most of northern and central Greece, including Athens, in 480. When Cyrus had defeated Croesus of Lydia 66 years earlier, and taken over his kingdom, its territory had included a number of major Greek settlements on the east coast of the Aegean, and more Greek cities had been incorporated into the empire through Cambyses' conquest of Cyprus. These cities were governed by individuals or small groups who were kept in power by the satraps and served their interests. In 499 many of them had risen in revolt from Persian rule, and they had been supported by a fleet of 20 ships sent from Athens, and five from Eretria, on the island of Euboea. The revolt had been put down by 494, and one of the largest Greek cities, Miletus, had been sacked. Included in the destruction was the major oracular shrine and temple of Apollo at Didyma.

Some years before the Ionian revolt, in the period *c.*511–506, Athens had gone through a period of civil unrest, involving the 'tyrant' Hippias, and two other men, Isagoras and Cleisthenes, who went on to establish the Athenian democracy. In the course of the struggle Isagoras had called in aid from Sparta, and in response Cleisthenes had opened negotiations with the Persians, through the satrap of Lydia, and possibly had gone as far as offering submission to the king. In Darius' eyes, therefore, Athens was a rebellious subject as much as the Ionian and Cypriote cities. In 492 the Persian general Mardonius had led a combined army and fleet across the Hellespont and through Thrace and Macedonia, with the intention of marching south to Eretria and

Athens, but the expedition had been called off when much of the fleet was wrecked off Mount Athos. Two years later Darius had sent another force, under Datis, across the Aegean. Many of the Greek islands had offered submission to the king, and Eretria had been sacked, but the army had been defeated by the Athenians at the battle of Marathon (490), bringing the campaign to an end.

After Darius' death, Xerxes had inherited his father's plans, and in 481 he marched with Mardonius along the same route that the general had previously taken. This time the campaign was a success in that Xerxes accepted the submission of all the Greek cities along his path, routed a small Spartan-led army at Thermopylae, and was able to sack Athens and carry trophies back from there to Susa. This success, however, was short-lived. Xerxes' fleet (which included significant numbers of Greek ships) was defeated by a Greek fleet at Salamis in 480, and his army was defeated at Plataea the following year and retreated back to Asia.

In the next few years the remaining Persian forces were driven from the north Aegean, and the Greek cities of western Anatolia were, for a few decades, liberated from Persian control, becoming instead members of an Athenian-led alliance. It was not long, however, before Persian authority was restored on the east Aegean coast. Increasing distrust between the Greek cities led eventually to the Peloponnesian War between Athens and Sparta and their respective allies (431–404), and the real victor of that conflict was the Achaemenid empire. Both sides had tried to win support from the Kings Artaxerxes I (465–424) and Darius II (423–405), and it was the intervention in particular of Darius' younger son Cyrus on the side of the Spartans that gave them the naval power they needed to force the Athenians to surrender. In return for that support the Spartans had agreed to give up the Greek cities on the Asian mainland to the Persians.

Relations between the Spartans and the Persians broke down on the death of Darius II, as Spartan officers with a body of mercenary soldiers supported Cyrus in an unsuccessful attempt to take the throne from his elder brother Artaxerxes II (405–359). This campaign was described by the Athenian writer Xenophon, who took part in it, in his *Anabasis*, a work that provided a model for Arrian's *Anabasis* of Alexander. Artaxerxes finally settled affairs in the Aegean area in 386 by an arrangement that was known as the King's Peace, in which Achaemenid rule over the cities of the Asian mainland was recognized, and the king threatened to intervene with troops or money if the Greeks of the islands and the European mainland did not respect the settlement and each other's autonomy. In the following decades Persian money was provided to leading Greek politicians to ensure that they advocated policies that did not conflict with the king's interests, and there was little direct conflict between Greeks and the forces of the Achaemenid empire.

## The Achaemenid empire in the 4th century

Xerxes' successors put up few royal inscriptions, and as a result we know much less about events elsewhere in the empire than we do for earlier periods. A Greek historian, Ctesias of Cnidus, spent time at the court of Artaxerxes II, and wrote a history of Persia now known only through quotation from other authors, but this does not tell us much. The empire remained mostly intact, although Egypt broke away from Achaemenid control in 404, and was only reconquered in 343, by Artaxerxes III (359–338). We know about the events of the last years of the empire from a number of Babylonian documents including the so-called *Dynastic Prophecy*, which reports some episodes of intrigue in the Achaemenid court. On the death of Artaxerxes III, possibly by poison but probably from natural causes, most of his relatives were murdered at the instigation of a court eunuch, Bagoas, and his one surviving son was installed as Artaxerxes IV (338–336). Two years later Bagoas had him too killed, and with the rest of the family already dead Bagoas installed a distant relative, Darius III (336–331), on the throne. Darius had been a successful military leader, and turned out to be the wrong choice for Bagoas, who was killed on the king's orders. This was the man who was to face Alexander the Great.

## Macedonia: the first 150 years

Meanwhile, in Macedon Amyntas' son, Alexander I (c.495–454), was able to hold on to his position after Xerxes' defeat in the Aegean. He became known as Alexander Philhellene ('Friend of the Greeks'), and Herodotus reports stories which present him as having secretly worked against the Persians all along. His kingdom faced challenges from all sides, and at times from within. The Macedonian heartland was the substantial plain at the northwest corner of the Aegean, through which the rivers Haliacmon and Axios flowed, known as Lower Macedonia, with its royal capital, Aegae, at the southern edge of the plain. Alexander I had extended his rule into the higher ground to the west and north (Upper Macedonia), and also eastwards to the valley of the Strymon, to control a territory of over 17,000 km² (that is a little larger than the historic county of Yorkshire in the UK, or a little smaller than the state of New Jersey in the USA). As well as including large amounts of fertile land for agriculture and stock rearing, the area had forests and deposits of silver and gold. It was, however, hemmed in on all sides by potential enemies. To the east were the kingdoms of Thrace while to the northwest and west lay Illyria and Epirus. On the Aegean coast, and in particular on the Chalcidice peninsula, there were Greek cities that had been established in the 7th and 6th centuries.

Macedonian kings sometimes made multiple marriages, and as a consequence tended to produce several sons with different mothers. This practice of polygamy allowed the king to make considerable use of marriage-alliances to seal diplomatic arrangements, and it meant that there was no shortage of male heirs. On the other hand it meant that the death of a king of Macedon more than once led to a period of instability as his heirs fought each other for the throne. This happened on the death of Alexander I, and his successor Perdiccas II (454–413) took several years to establish himself in power. His reign was characterized by frequent threats from his neighbours, dealt with by a combination of limited military action, not always successful, and negotiation.

His successor Archelaus (413–399) is credited with strengthening Macedonian military effectiveness, building roads and fortifications, and possibly introducing new infantry formations. He also built a new capital at Pella, in the Macedonian plain, and established a court which attracted Greek artists and writers, including the Athenian tragedian Euripides, to move there. After Archelaus' death there was more fighting amongst his successors until his cousin Amyntas III (393–369) was able to establish himself in power. His reign coincided with increased expansionism from Illyria and growing hostility from the Greek cities of Chalcidice. These pressures continued after his death, and new ones were added, as Macedonia started to be more directly involved in the affairs of the Greek cities further south. After Amyntas' death, his son Alexander II (369–368) campaigned in Thessaly before he was assassinated, and his successor, Ptolemy (368–365), who was probably acting as regent for Alexander's younger brother Perdiccas, allied the kingdom with the Greek city of Thebes, sending hostages, including the future Philip II, another brother of Alexander and Perdiccas, to Thebes as a sign of good faith. Under Perdiccas III (365–360) Macedon found itself for a while allied with Athens instead of Thebes, but the arrangement was short-lived, as was Perdiccas himself, who was killed in battle against an invading Illyrian army, leaving the throne to his brother Philip II (360–338), the father of Alexander the Great.

## Philip II

It took Philip less than three years to transform the fortunes of Macedonia through a combination of diplomacy, military reorganization, and skilled generalship. As well as having to deal with the advancing Illyrian army, he faced the threat of an uprising in Paeonia in Upper Macedonia and the possibility of a challenge for the throne from three half-brothers and two other pretenders, backed by Athens and Thrace. He was able to negotiate with the Athenians and bribe the Thracians to nullify this last danger, and he had his half-brother Archelaus executed. He also induced the Paeonians to end their threat by offering money, and was able to negotiate a temporary truce with the Illyrians. This gave him time to improve the training and organization of his army. There is some debate about how far Philip was responsible for innovations in the Macedonian way of fighting, and how much was achieved by his predecessors or left to his son Alexander to complete. Since this is a book about Alexander, it makes more sense to look at the army as it was under Alexander, and this will be described in Chapter 3. It is generally recognized, however, that Philip increased the effectiveness of the Macedonian armed forces by recruiting larger numbers of both infantry and cavalry, and instituting more regular and more thorough training. By 358 he was able to march against the Illyrians and to drive them out of Upper Macedonia.

Philip secured his relationship with his neighbours through a series of marriages. The first of his seven wives was Phila, from Elimiotis in Upper Macedonia; she was joined by Audata, a member of the Illyrian royal family, and two women from leading families from Greek cities in Thessaly, Nicepolis and Philinna, and then in 357 by Olympias, a member of the Epirote royal family. Later in his reign he married Meda, daughter of a Thracian king, and finally Cleopatra, a member of a high-ranking Macedonian family. Philip's father Amyntas III had six sons through two marriages. In contrast Philip's wives, who produced several daughters, bore him only two sons: Philinna gave birth to Arrhidaeus, who was for some reason considered unfit to rule, and Olympias was the mother of Alexander the Great. Royal wives who did not have sons had little influence at court, and little is known about these various women. Olympias, however, lived through Alexander's reign, and wielded considerable influence. We will learn more about her in the next chapter.

Philip's activities after this make it clear that he saw aggression as the most effective way to secure Macedonian interests, but he accompanied it with other activities which demonstrated that he could work with the Greeks as well as against them. In the period 357–354 he took control of all of the Greek cities in the region outside Chalcidice, from Amphipolis in the east to Pydna in the south. He also took over the city of Crenides, which controlled very productive gold and silver mines, and renamed it Philippi. In 356 he entered a chariot in the Olympic Games, and won. This was more than mere display: Olympic victors were recognized in Greece as having the favour of Zeus, and were treated with particular respect, so Philip's victory made him more difficult to ignore.

In 356 a war broke out in central Greece between Phocis and Boeotia, partly over control of the sanctuary and oracle of Apollo at Delphi. Modern scholars know it as the Third Sacred War. The cities of Thessaly, which lay between Macedonia and Phocis, became involved in the war, and Philip was called on by Larissa, the home city of his wife Philinna, to defend it against the Phocians who supported its rival Pherae (home city of another of his wives, Nicepolis—it is possible that the marriage took place after these events). In 352 Philip defeated the Phocians, and was elected commander of the whole of Thessaly. Gradually he was being drawn into the affairs of the major Greek cities.

Involvement in the south alternated with aggressive advances to the east. Philip returned to Macedonia, and went to war with king Cersobleptes of Thrace, and then moved against Chalcidice, capturing the most powerful Greek city there, Olynthus, in 348. Then in 346 he marched back south into Phocis, occupied the pass of Thermopylae, where Xerxes had defeated the Spartans, which controlled land routes between central Greece and the north, and brought the ten-year war with the Boeotians to an end. The sanctuary of Apollo at Delphi, along with the area around Thermopylae, was overseen by a council of Greeks known as the Delphic Amphictyony, made up of delegates mainly from the area around the sanctuary ('*amphictyon*' means 'neighbour'). It was not entirely clear before this date who was entitled to membership of the council, but as part of the settlement after the war, the Phocians were expelled from it, and Philip took their place. It is also unclear what influence the council had—its main task was to oversee the festival of the Pylaea, celebrated twice a year at Thermopylae, and to protect the sanctuary at Delphi—but, like his Olympic victory, membership of the Delphic Amphictyony made Philip an honoured individual in the eyes of many, if not all, Greeks. Following this he returned to Thrace, annexing Cersobleptes' kingdom by 342, and marching north as far as the Danube.

What Philip's ultimate aims were at this point is something that modern scholars disagree about, and it was unclear to his contemporaries as well. The larger Greek cities of the south, including Athens and Sparta, had interests in the natural resources of the north Aegean area, and at times formed alliances with both the northern Greek cities and the Thracian kingdoms: the growth of Macedonia could be seen to threaten their interests. The Athenians in particular were dependent on supplies of grain from the Black Sea, and so could not have a hostile power controlling the Bosporus or Hellespont. Philip's advance eastwards was also a potential threat to the Persian king. By 340 Philip was besieging cities on the north shore of the Sea of Marmara, including Byzantium, and Artaxerxes III sent supplies and mercenary troops to support them. He also, like his predecessors, sent money to politicians in Athens and elsewhere to encourage them to oppose Philip wherever possible. On the other hand Philip had been invited to intervene in Thessaly and central Greece by the leaders of Greek cities who saw him as someone who could protect them against their rivals. It is quite possible that, having secured control of the areas around Macedonia, he wanted to maintain peaceful relations with the other Greeks. Some Athenian politicians and pamphleteers, probably the recipients of gifts from him, argued for supporting Philip in a campaign against the Persians; others, equally probably receiving money from Artaxerxes, took an opposite view.

Events at opposite corners of the Aegean led to the final confrontation between Philip and Athens that brought his campaigns in Greece to completion. In 340 the Athenians made an alliance with Byzantium, which was under siege by Philip. He responded by seizing the Athenian grain fleet, and the Athenians declared war. Later that year the Delphic Amphictyony accused the city of Amphissa, just west of Delphi, of cultivating land sacred to Apollo, and began a military campaign against it. When the first season's campaign did not lead to a settlement, Philip was called down to deal with the problem. He marched against Amphissa, and then turned west to threaten Athens. Demosthenes, Athens' most effective orator, and one of the recipients of gifts from the Persian king, encouraged the Athenians to march out against Philip, and persuaded the Thebans to join them. The two sides met at Chaeronea in August 338, and Philip was the victor. He installed a garrison in Thebes, but made no attempt to punish the Athenians. Instead, he started to organize his next campaign.

In the Spring of 337 representatives of all the Greek cities except Sparta gathered at Corinth and swore oaths of allegiance to Philip, establishing an organization called by modern scholars the League of Corinth. At the meeting Philip announced a planned invasion of the Achaemenid empire, with the avowed aims of punishing the Persians for the destruction caused by Xerxes, and of once more liberating the Greek cities of Asia. To muster all the troops required for the campaign would take time, but in March 336 a Macedonian advance force of 10,000 men, led by Philip's generals, Parmenion and Attalus, crossed the Hellespont from Europe into Asia.

# Chapter 2

# Prince: Alexander in the Macedonian court

Alexander the Great was born in July 356, in the royal palace in Pella, while his father Philip II was campaigning against the Greek cities in the Chalcidice peninsula. As is to be expected in the case of a man whose achievements were to be so impressive, stories of omens surrounding his birth later circulated widely. The temple of Artemis at Ephesus supposedly burned down on the day Alexander was born, and it was suggested that Artemis, who was associated with child-birth among other things, had neglected her temple because she was attending the Macedonian prince's birth. It was also said that Philip received the news of Alexander's birth on the same day that he also learned that his chariot had won the Olympic Games, and that his general Parmenion had defeated the Illyrians. On the basis of this coincidence, seers were said to have predicted that Alexander would be 'invincible' or 'unconquered' (the Greek word is *aniketos*). This is a word that was frequently used to describe him by later writers.

Of the Alexander historians only Plutarch has anything to say about his childhood. Some of what Plutarch says is supported by other writers, in particular his account of Alexander's education under the guidance of the philosopher Aristotle, but several of the more dramatic stories seem to be included because they foreshadow Alexander's later achievements rather than because they are reliable. These include the story of how Alexander came to master his horse, Bucephalas, which was considered to be impossible to control, after he made a bet with his father that he could do this. Alexander does appear to have had particular affection for this horse, and is said to have offered a huge reward for its return when it was stolen in northern Iran. After the horse died during Alexander's campaigning in the Punjab, he named a city that he founded in the region Bucephala in its memory. The question of whether the story of his taming Bucephalas explains this affection, or whether the story was inspired by Alexander's later actions, remains open.

## Royal women

For the Greeks and Macedonians of Alexander's time, and the Greeks and Romans of the time of the Alexander historians, an orderly society was one where decisions were taken by men. It was acceptable for women to protect the interests of their children, particularly their sons, by appealing to the male members of their families, but not to act on their own behalf. Greek literature as far back as the poems of Homer offered positive images of women who could influence their husbands to show kindness to strangers, or respect to the gods, but it also presented negative images of dangerous women who challenged the proper order of things. In democracies women's influence was necessarily limited, but in monarchies the women of the royal family could have considerable indirect power, and would be expected to use it on their children's behalf. Macedonia was no exception.

Plutarch tells a number of stories about Alexander's mother Olympias, with whom he had a close relationship throughout his life. Even while he was on campaign they corresponded by letters, and he sent gifts back to her from the spoils of his victories. Plutarch's stories are not favourable to Olympias: she is presented as jealous and suspicious in her relationship with Alexander's father Philip, and also as wild and dangerous. Part of the explanation for this is that Olympias was involved in the competition and conflict between Alexander's successors after his death, and various individuals had reasons to present a negative picture of her. It is difficult to know where the truth behind these depictions lies, but it is possible to get a more balanced understanding of the place of women in the Macedonian court by looking at the experience of other royal women. What we can say about Alexander's grandmother Eurydice and his sister Cleopatra can help us understand more about his mother.

## Eurydice

The career of Eurydice, wife of Amyntas III and mother of Philip II, who may well have been alive during Alexander's early childhood, demonstrates what women could achieve, and what they might have to endure, both in life and in reputation. Eurydice was either Illyrian or Lyncestian, and Amyntas married her to maintain good relations with potentially dangerous neighbours. She bore him three sons, and this, more than anything else, will have raised her status in the Macedonian court. When Amyntas died, Eurydice was forced to enter the world of diplomacy. Her eldest son Alexander II was at this point already dead or else on the frontier fighting against the Illyrians, while a pretender, Pausanias, was making a rapid advance into Macedonia. Eurydice took her younger sons, Perdiccas and Philip, and went to the Athenian general Iphicrates, who was in the region trying to take control of the Greek city of Amphipolis. Iphicrates had been adopted by Amyntas, so Eurydice could claim him as her own step-son. According to the Athenian orator Aeschines, Eurydice put her sons into Iphicrates' lap, and begged him to protect them as his brothers. The appeal to family ties made what might otherwise have been an inappropriate action for a woman acceptable, and Iphicrates drove Pausanias out of Macedonia. A less reliable story has Eurydice, not long after this, marrying a man called Ptolemy, who had successfully installed himself as regent for Perdiccas, so that she could continue to protect her sons' interests. Who this Ptolemy was is uncertain, but it has been suggested that he was her son-in-law, who had killed her son Alexander II. If so, then Eurydice was marrying the killer of one of her sons to protect the others. An even more lurid version of events is told by Justin: he claims that Eurydice, out of a desire to marry Ptolemy, had attempted unsuccessfully to murder Amyntas, and that after his death she herself had first had Alexander and then Perdiccas killed. Aeschines' sympathetic story was told less than 30 years after the events, whereas Justin's source, Pompeius Trogus, was writing over 300 years later, with a Roman's distaste for women intervening in political affairs, but Justin's version of events was, until recently, accepted as fact. The way in which Eurydice was transformed by ancient and modern scholars from a mother relying on family connections to protect her sons into an ambitious schemer prepared to kill them should give us pause when we consider the accounts of her daughter-in-law, Olympias, mother of Alexander the Great.

## Cleopatra

It was at the wedding of Alexander's sister to her uncle, Olympias' brother, generally referred to as Alexander of Epirus, that their father Philip was assassinated. Cleopatra, like Olympias, received gifts from Alexander's spoils, and at some point she interceded with him on behalf of a local dynast in Anatolia, not an inappropriate action for a sister. Alexander of Epirus died on campaign in Italy, leaving a son Neoptolemus, and a daughter, Cadmeia, and Cleopatra acted as regent for them: Neoptolemus did become ruler of Epirus some 30 years later. As Philip's daughter Cleopatra became a potentially valuable wife for the generals competing for power after Alexander's death, but she was eventually killed under uncertain circumstances in 308 BCE, when she was around 50 years old. Her life, like that of her grandmother, for all that it gave her important responsibilities, was defined by her relationships to the male members of her family.

# Olympias

Olympias' career was not very different from those of her mother-in-law and her daughter. She was the daughter of Neoptolemus of Molossia, in Epirus, and her marriage to Philip was, as usual, arranged for diplomatic reasons. As the mother of Alexander her standing in the court will have been high, but little is reported about her in the period before Alexander became king—and that little is likely to be fantasy rather than fact. The story of the birth of Alexander became associated with miraculous events, and over time even stories about his conception grew up. A tradition, probably originating in Egypt in the 3rd century, claimed that Alexander was the son of Zeus, or the Egyptian god Amun, who came to Olympias in the form of a snake. Plutarch reports this story, but offers what appears to be a rationalizing explanation for it: Olympias was, he says, like most women in the region, a devotee of Orphic and Bacchic rites—that is the ecstatic worship of the god Dionysus—and she provided large snakes for these rites. It is true that the story of the death of Orpheus, torn apart by maenads or bacchants, devotees of Dionysus, was traditionally associated with Macedonian Pieria, and that Euripides' tragedy, *Bacchae*, in which the king of Thebes, Pentheus, is killed by his mother and other women in a maenadic frenzy, was first performed in Macedonia at the court of Archelaus. It is also the case that Dionysiac imagery is found on some of the magnificent vessels buried in 4th-century Macedonian tombs. But even if Olympias did take part in Bacchic rituals, which is by no means certain, and even if they did involve handling snakes, which is less likely, the resulting image of Olympias as snake-obsessed is pure invention. In those places where we have clear evidence of women taking part in Bacchic activities (and they do not include Macedonia in this period), the women who acted as priestesses were not seen as deviant in their behaviour.

After Philip's death, Olympias, as queen mother, continued to have an important role at the court in Macedon, while Alexander was on campaign. Plutarch and Arrian both refer to correspondence between Alexander and Olympias, although the texts they had access to are generally reckoned not to be genuine. It is probable that she did not have a good relationship with Alexander's regent, Antipater, and she moved back to Molossia around 330. After Alexander's death, Olympias' position became dependent on the fortune of Alexander's infant son, Alexander IV, and she was part of his entourage when she was killed by Cassander, Antipater's son, in 315. Like her mother-in-law, Eurydice, Olympias is depicted negatively in the surviving narratives; but attempts to invert these accounts to present Olympias as a powerful and independent woman are not necessarily any closer to the truth. Her position, like Eurydice's, depended on her son, and later her grandson. If we could get to a true picture behind the misleading representation of the surviving ancient narratives, which we cannot, it is likely that we would find that she was neither heroine nor monster, but that she fulfilled the expected role of a woman in Macedonian society, dutifully working for her children, at whatever cost.

## The life of a prince

Archaeological excavation at the royal sites of lower Macedonia in the last few decades has done more than anything else to cast light on the world in which Alexander grew up. Although Alexander was born in Pella, which had been the royal centre of Macedon since the end of the 5th century, it is the excavations at the palace and tombs at Aegae, near modern Vergina, that have expanded the understanding of Macedonian public life in his time.

The palace at Aegae was probably built by Philip II. It stood on an outcrop of rock on the slope of the hill that formed the acropolis of the ancient city of Aegae, dominating the city below it with a monumental entrance facing the city. At the centre of the palace was an open area surrounded by a peristyle. In this open court the king could address his courtiers, and in the rooms that opened off the peristyle they could dine in groups of up to 30. Some of the mosaic floors of the palace survive, showing that it was richly decorated, but inevitably the wall decorations and the contents of the building have not survived. However, something of their wealth and splendour can be guessed at from what was found in the most famous archaeological discoveries at the site of Vergina-Aegae, the Macedonian royal tombs. These tombs, one of which may be that of Philip II, contained rich grave goods including furniture decorated with gold and ivory, as well as jewellery and other ornaments of gold and silver. Elsewhere in Macedonia other rich burials have been excavated, packed with vessels of gold, silver, and bronze. The royal tombs were painted with scenes from myth and from court life, and the palace will have been decorated in the same way. One theme of Macedonian art is particularly worth noting, and that is the Royal Hunt.

## Hunting

There is no doubt that hunting was an important part of Macedonian elite life. In his collection of texts about eating and drinking, *The Learned Banqueters*, the writer Athenaeus of Naucratis includes the statement from a 3rd-century historian Hegesander, that no Macedonian was permitted to recline at dinner unless he had killed a wild boar without the use of nets. One of the plots against Alexander from within his court started after Alexander had one of his pages flogged, because, during a hunt, he killed a boar which Alexander was about to claim for himself. A successful boar hunt marked a transition between boy and man, and so for Alexander to dishonour a youth who had just made that transition by beating him was a particularly humiliating act. Hunting was a frequent subject of Macedonian art. Mosaics from Pella, and the largest painting from the royal tombs at Vergina-Aegae depict Philip and Alexander hunting lions, either on horseback or on foot. Mountain lions could be found in Macedonia in that period, but lion hunts will have been less common than boar hunts. It is likely that one of the reasons for depicting lions was emulation of Persian, and before them Assyrian, kings, who decorated their own palaces with scenes of lion hunts, and close combat between the king and one or more lions. As he advanced through the territories of the Achaemenid empire Alexander visited and hunted in some of the hunting parks created by satraps and by previous kings.

As we have seen, the early history of the Macedonian monarchy was linked to the campaigns of the Persian king Darius in the north Aegean area. Even after Persian forces had left Europe at the end of Xerxes' unsuccessful invasion, the courts of the Persian satraps in Asia Minor remained powerful models for the monarchs of Thrace and Macedonia just to their west. It has been argued by some scholars that Philip II, even while he planned his campaign against the Persian empire, was prepared to emulate some of the Great King's court practices. He introduced the practice of aristocrats sending their young sons to the palace to serve as pages, and especially to accompany the king when he went hunting; the 4th-century historian Xenophon describes the Persian king as being accompanied in the same way. Alexander's upbringing will have prepared him well not only for ruling Macedonia, but for dealing with the powerful empire to its east.

## Alexander becomes king

Alexander's life in the Macedonian court was interrupted when he went into exile in Illyria after quarrelling with his father, who had recently married his last wife, Cleopatra, a Macedonian woman, the daughter of one of Philip's generals, Attalus. Plutarch, who reports the incident, implies that Alexander's position as Philip's heir was under threat, although this seems unlikely. Alexander returned to Macedon not long after this, in time to be present at his sister's wedding to her uncle, Alexander of Epirus. The wedding was celebrated with a great festival at Aegae, to which ambassadors from the Greek cities were invited. It was at this wedding that Alexander's father Philip was assassinated.

The killer was arrested before he could escape. He was one of Philip's bodyguards, called Pausanias, and it is possible that his motives were entirely personal. There were, however, inevitably many suggestions that he was part of a larger conspiracy. Two men from the leading family of Lyncestis in Upper Macedonia, Heromenes and Arrhabaeus, were accused of involvement in the plot, and executed alongside Pausanias, although their brother Alexander was not implicated. Alexander the Great is said later to have accused the Persian king Darius of plotting to assassinate Philip: his death would certainly have served Darius' interests, but no ancient writer appears to have made a connection between him and Pausanias. An alternative theory that Plutarch suggests was spread at the time was that Olympias was behind the assassination, and Justin implicates Alexander himself in the plot. It is difficult to see how Philip's death at this point would have benefited Alexander, however. Nor is it plausible that Olympias would have acted for Alexander without his knowledge. There is much that remains unclear about the death of Philip, but it left Alexander as heir to all his father's positions, above all as king of Macedon, and as leader of a proposed Greek expedition to seek for revenge against the Persians for the destruction they caused in 481–479.

# Chapter 3
## Warrior: Alexander's army

Alexander was engaged in military campaigning throughout his reign. Before he led his army against the Persian empire he had to deal with uprisings in the areas to the northeast and west of Macedonia, and then with the Greek city of Thebes, which he besieged and sacked. After crossing into Asia he fought three major pitched battles against the Persians, at the Granicus River (334), at Issus (333), and at Gaugamela (331), as well as one against the Indian king Porus on the Hydaspes River (326), and a number of smaller engagements. He successfully besieged a series of cities on the west coast of Anatolia and in the Levant. He was also faced with a long insurgency in Afghanistan (329–326), and more trouble in Pakistan during his march down the Indus Valley. He was, in the end, always successful. We have seen that the title of 'undefeated' became attached to him: it was well-deserved.

Many books have been written about Alexander's generalship and his armed forces, illustrated with plans of his various battles. However, the evidence on which these accounts and plans are based is not easy to use, and there is much about Alexander's achievements that remains guesswork. Even though Arrian himself had experience of military command, and wrote works on tactics, the ancient accounts of Alexander's battles and sieges were less concerned with the details of military formations and command structures, and more interested in illustrating the less tangible aspects of warfare.

## Forces

Some basic information about Alexander's army can be taken as reliable. He crossed into Asia to begin his campaign with around 32,000 infantry and 5,000 cavalry. There he joined up with the force of around 10,000 that Philip had sent out two years earlier. Seven thousand of the infantry and 600 of the cavalry were from the Greek cities of the League of Corinth, a further 5,000 infantrymen were Greek mercenaries, and the rest were Macedonians and their allies. The Greek cities also contributed ships to Alexander's fleet, but he was to disband this before the end of the year. As his campaign went on Alexander lost men to disease and to death and injury in battles and sieges, and through retirement, but he received a regular supply of reinforcements from Macedonia and Greece, and later on from within his newly conquered empire. Numbers provided by the ancient narratives for the size of his army remain generally consistent and believable throughout. The same cannot be said for the figures for the size of the armies he faced. At the battle of Gaugamela, for example, his second and final encounter with Darius III, figures for the Persian army range between 200,000 and 1,000,000 infantry and between 40,000 and 200,000 cavalry. Modern writers generally consider the likely number to have been below 100,000 men in total.

Alexander inherited his army from his father Philip, and its basic elements are referred to by enough ancient writers for us to understand its broad composition. The evidence from archaeology, in particular from grave goods, also helps our understanding of weapons and armour. There were cavalrymen armed with lances (but riding without stirrups, a fact which limited the impact with which they could charge); at the heart of the infantry was the so-called Macedonian phalanx, armed with

6-metre long pikes, called *sarissas*, and they are generally thought to have been flanked by men armed with thrusting spears and swords, and large round shields, like the hoplites of the Greek city states. As well as these there were light-armed troops, armed with javelins, bows, or slings. But attempts at greater specificity run into the problem that the ancient writers give a number of names for more specific units, without explaining what they are, and possibly sometimes using the same name for different units, or different names for the same units. The men of the phalanx are referred to as *pezhetairoi* ('foot-companions'), but there are also references to *asthetairoi*: it is not certain what this word means. Similarly the hoplites may be called *hypaspists* ('shield-bearers'), but towards the end of the campaign we have references to *argyraspids* ('silver-shields'), who may be an elite group of these men or something different. Such uncertainties do not cause major problems in the reconstruction of battles, but they have generated a small scholarly industry of attempts to work out what the terms referred to.

Ancient armies were made up of more than their soldiers, and the presence of camp-followers is occasionally noted by the ancient writers. Every cavalryman would have had an attendant, and although Philip is supposed to have limited infantrymen to one servant for every ten soldiers, officers would have had more. As the campaign progressed, soldiers would acquire booty, and need slaves to look after it and them. There were also, no doubt, numerous other camp-followers offering their services, of many kinds, for food or pay. Periodically attempts were made to reduce the amount of baggage and the number of hangers-on, but as war-fighting was a recognized means of acquiring possessions much of the time the camp-followers must have outnumbered the soldiers.

## Sieges

Alexander's forces also included a siege train. This was an aspect of warfare that Alexander appears to have developed considerably:

catapults, battering rams, and siege towers, dismantled and loaded onto mule carts, would follow behind the army, along with the rest of the baggage train. The 7-month siege of Tyre (332) was one of his most celebrated achievements in antiquity. This is clear from the detailed accounts that we have of it, not only in the surviving historians, but also in the *Alexander Romance*, the popular version of Alexander's life that circulated widely, and was continually embellished, in the ancient and medieval worlds. And it is one case where Alexander's actions left a permanent mark on the landscape. The ancient city of Tyre was built on an island just off the Lebanese coast. During the siege Alexander built a causeway out towards the island, and although it was not completed, it led to the subsequent silting up of the channel in between, and so the ruins of ancient Tyre, such as they are, are now part of the mainland.

## Battles

When it comes to reconstructing Alexander's battles, the starting point is the accounts in the surviving sources. These can be supplemented by autopsy: modern writers have visited the sites of the battles—although ancient accounts of the topography are not always precise, and in some cases it has proved difficult to identify where encounters took place. For example, the 'Persian Gates', where an Achaemenid force tried to prevent Alexander getting through the Zagros Mountains to Pasargadae and Persepolis, has not been satisfactorily located. But even when we have several descriptions of a battle, and a good idea of where it was fought, there are severe problems facing any attempt at a detailed reconstruction. Ptolemy, the historian on whose work Arrian and Plutarch draw, probably took part in all the major battles of the campaign. And yet this would not necessarily make him a good source of information. From his position somewhere in the cavalry, he would only have seen a small part of the action, and most of this would have been confused and confusing. But in any case it is likely that Ptolemy did not rely primarily on his own memory for reconstructing events. He probably based his battle descriptions on those of Callisthenes, Alexander's 'official historian', who may have witnessed the battles from a distance, and who would have been able to talk to a range of participants. But Callisthenes may not have been concerned with accuracy above all, as a consideration of the accounts of Alexander's first battle against the Persians, at the Granicus River, will show.

## The Battle of the Granicus

According to Arrian and Plutarch, Alexander marched from Troy, where he had visited the tomb of Achilles, and had taken from the temple of Athena a shield supposedly used in the Trojan War, to the River Granicus where he had found a Persian force commanded by the local satraps holding the far bank, which was high and steep. Parmenion, the senior member of his staff, suggested that Alexander should postpone his attack until the morning, but Alexander is said to have responded that the Hellespont would be ashamed if, after he had crossed it, he was now held up by the trickle that was the Granicus, and with that he led his troops into the river and against the Persians. Arrian gives rather more details about what happened next, but both authors include a list of Persians whom Alexander met and killed, one after another, once he had gained dry land on the far side. It has been recognized that this is the most difficult of Alexander's battles to reconstruct, because the description is rather vague, and scholars have commented that the series of single combats fought by Alexander resembles passages from Homer's *Iliad* more than anything else. The resemblance to Homer may in fact have been deliberate, especially if it is Callisthenes' account that is being followed here. Early in the description of Achilles' one day of fighting in the *Iliad*, Homer describes how the hero leaps into the river Scamander in pursuit of the Trojans, and battles with the river itself. Alexander claimed descent from Achilles, and Callisthenes' description of the battle—first the leap into the river, and then the sequence of single-combats—will have been as much influenced by a wish to bring out the relationship between the two heroes as by any concern for accurate reportage. Diodorus gives a rather different account of the battle, in which Alexander camped overnight near the river and was then able to bring his troops over unopposed early in the morning, and fight on dry land. Whatever Diodorus' source was, in this case his version may be nearer the truth.

If Diodorus was more accurate, then one of the elements in the other version that has to be rejected is the exchange between Alexander and Parmenion about the wisdom of launching an attack across the river. There are several such exchanges described between the two men in the surviving narratives, and they have a standard pattern: Parmenion offers sensible, if cautious, advice to Alexander; he ignores it, and turns out to be right to do so. Often, the exchanges are occasions for wit: when Darius sent a letter to Alexander offering peace terms, Parmenion is said to have remarked 'I would accept, if I were you', to which Alexander responded, 'so would I, if I were you.' There is no reason to assume, as some have done, that these stories reflect a growing rift between the two men. It is true that Alexander had Parmenion killed, after his son was convicted of plotting against the king, but up until that point Parmenion remained a trusted adviser, and was given rich rewards by Alexander. It is better to recognize that these are examples of a particular kind of story, that of the 'wise adviser'. These stories depict an older man giving advice to a young ruler, so in Herodotus' *Histories* the young Cyrus the Great is given advice by Croesus, former king of Lydia, and Xerxes is given advice by his uncle Artabanus, and by the former king of Sparta, Demeratus. Normally the young man, if he is wise, accepts the advice and prospers, or, if he is foolish, rejects it and suffers. But the stories involving Alexander reverse this pattern: he rejects the advice and still prospers, revealing that he is a truly exceptional ruler. The ancient writers use their narratives to illustrate their conception of Alexander's character, sometimes at the expense of fidelity to the facts.

There were other ways of heightening the significance of Alexander's achievements in battle. The narrative of Xerxes' invasion of Greece, as told particularly by Herodotus, offered the historians of Alexander an opportunity to draw parallels between the two commanders. The clearest example of this is the description of Alexander's entry into the province of Fars, where the city and palace of Persepolis was located, through a pass in the Zagros Mountains known as the Persian Gates.

## The Persian Gates

As Xerxes marched through Greece towards Athens in 480, the only place where he could be stopped was a narrow passage between the mountains and the sea in central Greece called Thermopylae, a name meaning 'Hot Gates', so-called because of a local hot spring. Herodotus describes how the pass was defended by the Spartan king Leonidas and 300 Spartan hoplites, supported by some 5,000 other troops. According to his account the Spartans, who could have held out indefinitely, were betrayed by a local man called Ephialtes, who led a party of Xerxes' troops along a little-known path that took them behind the Spartan position. On the third day of the battle, Leonidas found his troops surrounded, and he died on the battlefield. Xerxes' victory left the path to Athens open, and he was able to sack the city not long after. Although the battle ended in an avoidable defeat—Leonidas knew about the path, but did not protect it adequately—it quickly came to be considered an example of heroic self-sacrifice, and this is how Herodotus, writing around 50 years later, describes it, and how it has entered popular culture. But the narrative could also be reused.

The historians all describe Alexander's advance from Mesopotamia towards Fars through the Zagros Mountains, which involved going through a narrow pass referred to by Diodorus as the Susian Rocks, but by Arrian as the Persian Gates, held against him by a Persian commander, Ariobarzanes. Like Leonidas at the

Hot Gates, Ariobarzanes had built a wall across the pass to protect his forces, but his forces were much greater, at 25,000 infantry according to Diodorus, and 40,000 according to Arrian—although as always these figures are unreliable and implausibly high. The authors describe how, after at first failing, like Xerxes, to break through the enemy position by a frontal attack, Alexander was told by a local man about a narrow path through the mountains that would bring him out behind the Persian lines. In the fighting that followed, the Persians were defeated, but unlike Leonidas, Ariobarzanes ran away. This was Alexander's last military encounter on his way to Persepolis, which he destroyed (see Chapter 6) in revenge for Xerxes' sack of Athens after Thermopylae. The similarities between the accounts of the battles at the Hot Gates and the Persian Gates are too great to be coincidental, and it is clear that whatever may have actually happened in the Zagros Mountains, it suited those who wrote about it to present it as an appropriate inversion of Xerxes' sole victory in Greece.

## Omens

Another important area where the concerns of ancient writers differ from those of their modern successors is in their attention to supernatural aspects of warfare. As a modern discipline, military history tends to focus on practical issues—the relative strength and quality of opposing forces, the nature of terrain, logistical organization, the competence of commanders and their subordinates. While the ancient accounts of Alexander's campaigns are sometimes frustratingly lacking in these details, they are generally rich in accounts of omens and the advice of seers. This emphasis does reflect important truths about ancient warfare: given the uncertainty of war in general, ancient military commanders made considerable use of divination, looking to the gods to provide information that human resources could not. As a result, good *manteis* (seers), which means men who could not only correctly advise on the outcome of future actions, but who also had a record of being on the victorious side, were highly valued, and could expect rich rewards from the individuals and communities they served.

In the surviving accounts of Alexander's campaigns, above all in Arrian, his *mantis*, Aristander of Telmessus, plays a very visible role, interpreting a great variety of things, including the entrails of sacrificed animals, the behaviour of birds, dreams, astrological events like eclipses, and unusual phenomena such as sweating statues. All these are matters on which a seer would normally be consulted, but the stories need to be treated with care. It is a feature of ancient narratives, including historical ones, that prophecies always come true, one way or another. In Arrian and Plutarch, Aristander's predictions, however unlikely, always turn out to be correct, and it is clear that once again their inclusion in the narrative serves mainly to make a point about Alexander. It is appropriate that the greatest general should be accompanied by the greatest seer, so Aristander's perfect record of prediction is a reflection of Alexander's own invincibility. Aristander is not present in accounts of Alexander's last year, presumably because he had actually died at some point in the campaign, but it is only once Aristander has left the story that Alexander starts to witness omens foretelling his own death—not all of which are understood at the time.

## The campaigns

Alexander's expedition in Asia can be divided into two clear stages. In the first of these he was acting as the leader of an alliance of Greek states aiming to liberate the Greek cities of Asia from Achaemenid control, and to take revenge on the Persians for Xerxes' invasion of Greece 150 years earlier. The first of these aims, the liberation of the Greek cities, was largely achieved in 334, the first year of the campaign, as Alexander marched south through Asia Minor before turning eastwards into central Anatolia. The Persians regained control of some of the cities that he had freed in the following year, but Alexander sent a force to deal with this, and by the end of 332, Persian power in the region was permanently ended. Revenge on the Persians ultimately took the form of the destruction of the city and palace of Persepolis in Fars. Alexander's route there was by no means direct, but made sense militarily. In part it was determined by the actions of his opponent Darius in defending his territory. Alexander had disbanded much of his fleet not long after the start of the expedition, and needed to prevent Darius from using sea power. This was achieved by taking control of the major harbours along the east coast of the Mediterranean. The narratives of the Alexander historians offer additional explanations for Alexander's campaign decisions, often in terms of Alexander's personal desires: these may be accurate, but it is not clear what access they had to the workings of Alexander's mind. The march down the Mediterranean coast brought Alexander to Egypt, and although entering Egypt led him away from Darius and from Fars, detaching the wealthy kingdom of Egypt from Darius' empire would have made the detour well worthwhile. Once he left Egypt in the first part of 331, Alexander's journey took him fairly directly over the Euphrates and Tigris, then down through Mesopotamia, by way of the royal capitals at Babylon and Susa, across the Zagros Mountains, and into Fars. Alexander entered Persepolis less than a year after leaving Egypt, and destroyed the palace a few months later. That this marked the end of the allied campaign is clear from Alexander's next actions. He sent home the allied contingents, richly rewarding them, but he allowed any of the Greeks who wished it to re-enlist as mercenary soldiers. Therefore the army which set off from Persepolis in the summer of 330 was now concerned solely with fulfilling Alexander's own aims.

The second part of the expedition took Alexander first in pursuit of Darius, whom he had already twice defeated. When Darius was assassinated on the orders of one of his subordinates, Bessus, he became Alexander's new target. The pursuit led Alexander into Bactria and Sogdiana, the northeastern corner of the empire, where the local elite were slow to accept the change of regime. Hence it took three years for Alexander to settle the region.

Alexander's next move, southeast into the Punjab and the Indus Valley, is best seen as a new campaign. How many of the troops that had crossed the Hellespont with Alexander in Spring of 334 were still with him eight years later we cannot tell: injured and aging soldiers will have been sent home to be replaced with reinforcements sent from Macedonia throughout this period. Most of the older officers had also either died or been left in positions further west, but Alexander's younger companions remained with him. The Indian campaign brought Alexander downriver to the Indus Delta and his first contact with a tidal ocean. The last phase of the journey was back through southern Iran to Fars, with a fleet also being sent up the Persian Gulf towards southern Mesopotamia. Alexander then spent the last 18 months of his life in what is now western Iran and eastern Iraq.

The rest of this book will not provide a detailed narrative of the expedition. Although the following chapters are organized roughly chronologically, they are more thematic, and make use of contemporary material to show how Alexander fitted into the world through which he travelled. The simplest way to follow Alexander's campaign is by using the map and the timeline provided at the front of this book.

# Chapter 4

# Commander: Alexander and the Greeks

At the battle of Chaeronea in 338, Alexander's father Philip had established Macedonia as the dominant power in the Greek world west of the Aegean. The ostensible aim of the campaign against the Achaemenid empire planned by Philip and carried out by Alexander was to liberate the Greek cities to the east of the Aegean. Although Alexander's progress took him far beyond the world of the Greeks, as he took control of the kingdoms of the Near East, his relationship with them remained crucial to the security of his reign. The narrative accounts of Alexander's life have something to tell us about his treatment of the Greek cities, and ancient orators and modern scholars have debated the question of whether Alexander was a liberator or an oppressor. We can gain a bit more understanding of the issues if we look beyond the narratives and consider what inscriptions put up by the cities themselves at the time can tell us about Alexander's actions and their impact.

## Autonomy and control

In order to understand Alexander's relationship with the Greek cities it is important to be conscious of two central issues. The first is the meaning of the word *autonomia* (autonomy), which was an important element in ancient Greek political vocabulary, and the other is the existence of factionalism and rivalry, which characterized the political life of almost all Greek cities.

*Autonomia* was not the same as independence: it meant operating under the city's own laws, and therefore was more to do with the internal administration than with involvement with other powers. But whether a city counted as autonomous might be a matter of perspective. The Greek cities of Asia Minor were from the middle of the 6th century subordinated to the Lydians, the Persians, the Athenians, the Spartans, and then the Persians again. In the 5th century, as allies of Athens (or members of the Athenian empire, to give a more negative perspective) these cities could be described as autonomous, but that autonomy was only guaranteed by Athenian naval power, and potentially the presence of Athenian garrisons, installed to protect the autonomy of the city (as defined by the pro-Athenian political leadership) from the threat of Persian-supported exiles seizing power. From the perspective of these pro-Persian citizens (or former citizens) the garrison would be a sign of lack of autonomy. There was, however, for these cities, no option of complete independence from outside interference. Only a very few Greek cities could be described as truly independent: until the battle of Chaeronea in 338, Athens, Thebes, and Sparta were the exceptions, and their relationship with the Macedonian kings remained somewhat different from those of other cities.

Competition was a central part of ancient Greek life. From the poems of Homer onwards rivalry for prestige was a driving force in the lives of the richer and more influential members of communities. The development of the institutions of the city-state, in particular citizen assemblies and law-courts, did nothing to weaken this competition, but rather provided an arena and a more defined set of rules under which it might take place. Political divisions in Greek cities were determined not so much by ideology as by the personal ambition of individuals. Even terms like 'democratic' and 'oligarchic', which were used by historians and philosophers in their discussion of civic strife, referred usually to more pragmatic distinctions (in the 5th century, supported by Athens or supported by Sparta), as Thucydides indicates in his dramatic description of the civil disorder that broke out in Corcyra in the early years of the Peloponnesian War. In smaller cities it was normal for ambitious would-be leaders to look for support—financial and occasionally military—from larger cities; and even in Athens the leading politicians were prepared to take money from external powers. Opposing demagogues would take money from Philip II and from the Persian king.

The inevitable result of this rivalry for power was the existence of political exiles. The losing faction at any one time would find themselves expelled from their city after being convicted of working against its interests, or else would leave to avoid the risk of being killed—whether as a result of judicial process or not. Deprived of their property they would either look for support from guest-friends in other cities while plotting their own return, or, if they had outstayed their welcome, they might seek service as mercenary soldiers. Exile was the experience of richer members of the community—the poorer people played a more passive role in political life, even in democracies.

## The League of Corinth

When he defeated the armies of Thebes and Athens at the battle of Chaeronea, Philip II treated the two cities somewhat differently. In Thebes, an ally that had broken its agreement, he installed a garrison of Macedonian troops and, it is assumed, had the leading politicians hostile to Macedonia sent into exile. As a consequence of the advocacy of the orator Demades, no Athenian politician was expelled, and Athens was left ungarrisoned; the city became an ally of Philip, a status that made clear that the city remained an autonomous entity, even while it set limits to Athenian freedom of military action.

In the following year a more general agreement was established with the Greek cities (other than Sparta), some of the details of which are known from Athenian inscriptions. The arrangement is known as the 'League of Corinth' and involved the creation of an alliance led by Philip to campaign against the Persians. According to a speech delivered in Athens a few years later, attributed to Demosthenes but not actually written by him, the terms of the alliance began with the statement that the Greek cities were to be free and autonomous. One of the fragmentary inscriptions relating to this includes the terms of the oath sworn by the Greek cities as part of the agreement. They swear not to interfere with the constitutions of their allies, nor to seize any of their territory, or take up arms against them, or to overthrow the kingdom of Philip and his heirs, and they will fight on behalf of any ally that is attacked. It also refers to a common council of the allies—which could be called upon if any member were deemed to have broken the terms of the agreement—and to Philip as *hegemon*, that is leader of the alliance: where Philip and his successors decided to go, the allies would have to follow. An even more fragmentary inscription from the beginning of Alexander's reign provides details of what the Athenians and Alexander are expected to provide for the troops the Athenians will supply on the campaign. When Philip was assassinated Alexander acted fast to renew the terms of the alliance, but in the following year it was tested by the revolt of Thebes, which took place while Alexander was securing his northern frontier.

## The sack of Thebes

We have detailed accounts of the revolt of Thebes from Diodorus and Arrian, and although there are differences between them, they make it clear that the revolt followed a pattern very similar to revolts against the Athenians described by Thucydides in the 5th century. The trigger for the revolt was the arrival of exiles, backed it would appear by Persian money, who murdered the pro-Macedonian politicians who had been in control since the defeat at Chaeronea. This made it difficult for the citizen body to avoid conflict with Alexander, who arrived in front of the city before the new political leaders had a chance to rally support from other cities. Alexander made short work of the siege, and then turned the decision about what to do with the Thebans over to the council of allies, as the terms of the League of Corinth indicated he should. It was inevitable that the delegates would support the punishment of the rebel city, and although the destruction of Thebes that followed may appear a brutal act, it was not different from the way Athens had treated some other Greek cities in the 5th century.

## The cities of Asia Minor and the islands of the east Aegean

When Alexander led his army into Asia the following Spring, his first task was to take control of the Greek cities there away from the Persian king. This was not a straightforward task, and something of what it involved can be understood by examining the experience of the city of Mytilene on Lesbos, which can be reconstructed from what is said in the surviving narratives and from the information from an inscription recording the settlement of affairs. As it happens Thucydides gave a detailed account of the difficulties faced by the people of Mytilene when the city revolted from Athens in 428–427: the revolt failed when the majority of the citizen body showed no enthusiasm for holding out against the Athenian fleet sent to force them back into alliance. A little less than a century later they faced a similar situation. The terms of the treaties arranged between the Greek cities and the Persian king in the early 4th century, which were considered by the Persians at least still to be in force, gave control of the cities on the mainland of Asia to the king. The islands were not covered by this, but the Persians clearly aimed to get or keep control of these.

In 334, when Alexander led his army into Asia, he made an agreement of some kind with those in power in the cities on

Lesbos, and sent a garrison force of mercenary soldiers to support the men friendly to him who were now controlling Mytilene. In the following Spring the Persian navy arrived off Lesbos and persuaded the other cities to come over to their side. Mytilene was besieged, and the citizens, who had little real choice, given the power of the Persian fleet, came to terms with the Persians, agreeing to send away the mercenaries supplied by Alexander and to abrogate the arrangement they had made with him by destroying the stones on which its terms had been recorded. They agreed also to let back in to the city the exiles (who had presumably left the city when Alexander's forces arrived), and to restore to them half the property that they had held when they left the city. The other half presumably stayed in the possession of the men who had supported Alexander, and had possibly themselves been in exile before his arrival. Arrian suggests that the terms of this agreement were not actually upheld by the Persians once they were back in control of the city. In the next year, 332, Alexander sent a general, Hegelochus, to regain control of the islands, and he recaptured the cities of Lesbos, including Mytilene. The terms of a new settlement are recorded on an inscription that does survive— itself an indication that they may have been honoured.

The surviving part of the inscription does not explain what the terms were on which the exiles might now return: it is quite likely that they were the same as those offered when the Persians took control the previous year. It does, however, go into great detail about the procedures for ensuring reconciliation between the two factions within the city, the returning exiles and those already in the city. It aims to prevent the use of the lawcourts to challenge the terms of the reconciliation, and it establishes a body of arbitrators drawn equally from the returned exiles and those already in the city. Modern scholars have disagreed over whether Alexander's actions were those of a liberator or of a new conqueror of these cities. The reality of his position, however, was not a choice between freeing the cities or oppressing them, but rather the need simply to prevent the divisions between the leading citizens causing instability and the opportunity for a return by the Persians. In the city of Ephesus Alexander had to step in to prevent bloodshed between the rival factions. Contemporary inscriptions from the island of Chios and the city of Priene on the mainland refer to similar attempts to settle disputes, and indicate that Alexander was engaged in a great deal of correspondence and arbitration in trying to bring lasting order to the cities of the eastern Aegean.

One indication that Alexander was successful is in the honours he received from the cities he passed through. In a number of places later inscriptions indicate the existence of festivals called Alexandreia, and priests and altars to Alexander *Basileus* (King) and *Ktistes* (Founder). By the end of the 6th century it had become a regular practice for a city to honour the man who had founded it by celebrating an athletic festival in his honour and offering sacrifices to him. If, as was usual before the 5th century, the founder had spent the remainder of his life in his new city and died there, he would be buried in the centre of the city and his tomb would be considered a sacred place. He would be treated in the same way as mythical heroes, like Orestes in Sparta and Theseus in Athens, whose supposed bones were found and brought to those cities for formal burial. But there was no very clear distinction between the kind of honours paid to a hero and those paid to a god. On a number of occasions in the 5th century those in control of a city might decide that a new person deserved to be recognized as their founder. Most significantly at the end of the Peloponnesian War the Spartans installed a new regime on the island of Samos after taking it from Athenian control. The new rulers decided to honour the Spartan commander Lysander as their new founder, and created a festival in his honour, and honoured him as a god, according to a 3rd century Samian historian. It was in line with this that cities set up cults of Alexander and maintained them in the following centuries. Of course it was those individuals who benefited from Alexander's settlement of Asia Minor who would have had most cause to introduce such honours. They served to bolster the position of Alexander's supporters for example by attributing to him, as founder, responsibility for the very existence of their city; but this is not to deny the sincerity of the actions.

At Priene an inscription records that Alexander dedicated the newly built temple of Athena (Figure 4). In other cities, too, new temples started to be built in the wake of Alexander's passage. At Miletus the oracular temple of Apollo at Didyma, destroyed by the Persians in 494, was restored, and the oracle could once again be consulted. Such developments were not necessarily immediate, but they are witness to a significant transformation of the fortunes of those Greek cities.

## Sparta

One Greek city stood aloof from the rest and from the Macedonians. Sparta had, until its defeat by the Theban general Epaminondas in 371, been one of the most powerful cities in Greece, directly controlling 40 per cent of the Peloponnese, and leading an alliance that covered most of the rest. Since then Sparta had lost much of its territory and all of its dominance. The Spartans refused to join the League of Corinth, or to serve with Alexander, and instead negotiated with Darius for financial support to lead an uprising in Greece. After an abortive attempt in Crete in 333–332, the Spartan king Agis launched his revolt in the Peloponnese in 331. Anti-Macedonian politicians were able to mount support for Agis in many Peloponnesian cities, but the Athenians did not join him, and the crucial city of Megalopolis in Arcadia in the southern Peloponnese also stayed loyal to Alexander. Agis was killed when the Macedonian regent Antipater led an army against him as he was besieging Megalopolis, and that marked the end of significant opposition to Alexander anywhere in Greece.

## Athens

Athens appears to have received more honours from Alexander than other cities did. After his first victory, at the Granicus,

4. Inscribed blocks from the temple of Athena at Priene. The first inscription records the dedication of the temple by Alexander the Great

Alexander chose to send his share of the battlefield spoils to Athens to be dedicated on the acropolis: three hundred suits of armour, displayed with a pointed message: 'Alexander the son of Philip and the Greeks, except the Spartans, [set up these spoils, taken] from the barbarian living in Asia.' When Alexander took over the royal palace in Susa he found there a pair of statues that the Athenians had erected in honour of the Tyrannicides, Harmodius and Aristogeiton, two men who had assassinated the brother of the last tyrant of Athens, and were held to be heroes of liberation. Xerxes had taken the statues home with him to Persia after the sack of Athens in 480 BCE, and, according to Arrian, Alexander now sent them back. When Alexander had the palace at Persepolis destroyed as the final act of the campaign of the League of Corinth, it was Xerxes' sack of Athens that was most obviously being avenged.

As in all Greek cities, as we have seen, the politicians of Athens were divided between those who supported Alexander and those who did not. After Alexander's first victory over Darius himself, at Issus, when Darius was no longer in a position to offer financial support to them, the anti-Macedonian politicians remained quiet until the year after Alexander's death. Under the leadership of the orator Lycurgus, the Athenians increased their state revenues and used the money to restore and improve civic buildings including the Theatre of Dionysus and the Stadium (restored again for the first modern Olympic Games in 1896); the practice was established of performing the plays of the great tragedians of the 5th century, Aeschylus, Sophocles, and Euripides, at the festival of the City Dionysia, and considerable attention was paid to the *ephebeia*, the training of young men. After the tension and danger of the period from before the battle of Chaeronea until the destruction of Thebes, Athens flourished while Alexander was on campaign in the east, benefiting from the wealth that came back from the Persian empire in the hands of discharged veterans returning home. Modern scholars sometimes suggest that the Athenians were continually looking for ways to oppose Alexander, but the evidence to support this view is difficult to identify.

In 324 Alexander returned victorious from his campaign in Pakistan, emerging from the desert of Gedrosia at the head of his army. While this caused concern for some officials in his empire who had used his absence to enrich themselves from public funds, it was treated as an occasion for celebration by those in power in the Greek cities, who sent embassies to Susa and Babylon to congratulate him. In Athens a decision was taken to honour Alexander with a statue bearing the inscription 'King Alexander, Invincible God'. There is no reason to believe that this did not reflect the popular view of Alexander at that point as more than a conquering hero, and there was no significant objection to the proposal, which is known from a fragment of a contemporary speech. Although Alexander is referred to as a god, the statue was not accompanied by the setting up of an altar or the appointment of a priest, so it is not the same as the cult offered by the cities of Asia Minor. Its rather extravagant description of Alexander could be justified by the claims made, amongst others, that in Pakistan Alexander had travelled further than the god Dionysus, and captured places that even Heracles had failed to capture. Similar decisions may have been taken by other Greek cities, but such evidence as we have is of questionable value.

## Exiles

One of Alexander's most controversial acts on his return from the east, at least in the eye of modern scholars, was to require Greek cities to take back their exiles. As we have seen, exiles were a problematic phenomenon for nearly all Greek cities. It was not normally possible for individuals to possess land in cities other than their own, so those in exile for any length of time had to find some way of supporting themselves. Among the higher social groups who made up the majority of political exiles, fighting as a hoplite soldier or a cavalryman was one of the few forms of employment available, and many of the mercenaries who had served with Alexander would have been exiled from their cities at some point. As part of his reorganization of his empire on his return from the east, Alexander required many of his satraps to disband their mercenary forces, and some solution had to be found to make sure that these men had somewhere to go. The best solution was for them to return to their cities and settle on land there.

Alexander followed an established practice of using a major panhellenic festival, in this case the Olympic Games of 324, as the occasion for announcing his decision. Every Greek city would send sacred ambassadors to the festival, and it was therefore the ideal place for communicating important information. Requiring cities to take back exiles was to interfere in their affairs, reversing decisions taken by their courts. As such it challenged their autonomy, but the surviving histories disagree over how far the Greek cities did object. For Athens it presented particular problems, because many Athenians owned plots of land on the island of Samos, from which the Samian owners had been expelled. Those Athenians potentially faced a substantial loss of income if the previous owners were able to return.

An inscription survives relating to implementation of the decree in the city of Tegea in the Peloponnese. This makes clear that there was an opportunity for the cities to negotiate on how the restoration would take place, and it also shows that the concern to ensure reconciliation between the exiles and those who had stayed behind, which we saw in the settlement of Asia Minor, was a major issue here too. The surviving part of the inscription describes the procedure for allocating houses and garden plots to returning exiles, who would have to recompense the existing owners for them. It also mentions a special court made up of jurors from outside the city who are to deal with disputes. This was not a crude or heavy-handed action by Alexander. Had the years after 324 been as peaceful for the Greek cities as the years before (at least since the defeat of Agis in 331), it might have been possible to judge the impact of the exiles decree. However, Alexander's death the following year and the subsequent wars, not only in Greece but across the whole of Alexander's former empire, created disorder on an even larger scale than had hitherto occurred.

Modern scholars, following the lead of the ancient narratives, have tended to see the imposition of the 'Exiles Decree' as an authoritarian act, forcing cities to take in their former enemies against their will. This view is part of a wider interpretation of Alexander as an oppressor whose promise of 'freedom for the Greeks' was never anything more than an empty slogan. There were no doubt people who lost out from Alexander's actions—not least those who had been comfortable working with their previous Achaemenid overlords—but the evidence of the inscriptions above all suggests that Alexander wanted a good relationship with the Greek cities, and the wealth that he released from the treasuries of the Achaemenid royal capitals was to enrich the cities of Asia Minor and the mainland hugely over the following decades and centuries.

# Chapter 5
# Pharaoh: Alexander and Egypt

Alexander entered Egypt late in 332, facing no opposition from the inhabitants or from the Persian satrap Mazaces, who had too few soldiers to attempt any resistance. This was the first of the major Near Eastern kingdoms to come under his control, with a system of government that had its roots in over two-and-a-half millennia of Pharaonic rule. The popular image of Egypt as an unchanging civilization should not, however, be exaggerated: the centuries before Alexander's arrival had seen many changes of rule since the end of the imperial period of the Late Bronze Age New Kingdom. The end of the New Kingdom had been followed by four centuries of the 'Third Intermediate Period' (1069–664), when the kingdom had been disunited and ultimately conquered by the Assyrians. Following that, Dynasty XXVI (664–525) had ruled Egypt until the Persian invasion under Cambyses, which had led to 120 years of Achaemenid rule. Egypt broke away from the Persian empire in 404, but was reconquered sixty years later, only twelve years before Alexander's arrival. The conflicts which led to these transfers of power left their mark on Egyptian society. Nonetheless rulers would adopt the practices and forms of representation used by their successful predecessors, as they attempted to confirm their authority, and so maintain the appearance of continuity.

For the surviving Alexander historians two events are of crucial importance in Alexander's time in Egypt: the foundation of the city of Alexandria and the visit to the oracle of Amun at Siwa. Arrian introduces his accounts of both these episodes saying that Alexander was seized by *pothos*, that is, overwhelming desire: these are actions driven by his own personal emotions rather than from any practical considerations. This interpretation has been largely followed in recent scholarship. The ancient writers disagree about the relative chronology of the two events, and this may add to a suspicion that one of them, the story of the foundation of Alexandria, is not all that it seems.

## Alexandria

In the period of the Roman empire Alexandria, on the Egyptian coast at the western edge of the Nile Delta, was one of the most important cities in the world. Already by the end of the 3rd century BCE it had grown through trade to become the largest city in the world, and in antiquity only Rome ever grew larger. It was a great centre of trade and a crucial point of contact between the Mediterranean world and the East. The Library at Alexandria gathered together all of Greek literature, and became a centre of science and scholarship. It was at Alexandria, about a century after the death of Alexander, that the first calculations of the circumference of the earth were made; the Jewish Bible was also translated into Greek there in the 3rd century, and it was mainly through this translation, known as the Septuagint, that the Hebrew biblical texts were known to early Christian writers.

All the ancient Alexander historians emphasize Alexander's personal involvement in the construction of Alexandria, suggesting that he determined where it would be built (after receiving advice in a dream, according to Plutarch) and how the walls and the major public buildings would be laid out. They also all provide versions of a prophetic story about the foundation. They say that the outline of the city was marked out using barley grains (either because this was the normal Macedonian practice, or because no chalk was available); and then, according to some versions, birds flocked down and ate the barley. The use of barley was interpreted to mean that the city was destined to grow rich from the fruits of the earth, but in the versions involving the birds, their arrival was taken to predict the fact that people would come to Alexandria from far and wide to settle. How much, if anything, of these accounts can be trusted? The answer is that possibly none of it can be.

After Alexander's death his body was sent west from Babylon for burial in Macedonia. En route it was captured by Ptolemy and brought to Egypt, where it was entombed in Memphis, not Alexandria. Memphis remained the administrative centre of Egypt under Ptolemy, who had taken control of Egypt as satrap on Alexander's death, until at least 311. In a document he composed in that year, known as the 'Satrap Stele' written in Egyptian, Ptolemy states that he moved to 'the Fortress of King Alexander, formerly known as Rakotis, on the shore of the Greek sea'. This event, 12 years after Alexander's death, and 20 years after he left Egypt, may mark the real beginning of Alexandria. Ptolemy proclaimed himself king in 304, and it is probably only after that point that the city began to become a major cultural centre. Its most famous buildings, the library and museum, are usually associated with Ptolemy's son and successor Ptolemy II Philadelphus (283–246). It is not clear from the text of the Satrap Stele whether the site was named 'the Fortress of King Alexander' before Ptolemy I moved there or whether it still had the Egyptian name Rakotis. Archaeology has provided little information about the earliest history of the site, since the ancient city is buried beneath the modern city and the sea, although excavation is ongoing, and something may emerge in the future. At the moment there is little contemporary evidence to support the idea that Alexander himself was responsible for much of what was to become the most important city to bear his name.

As his campaign took him into eastern Iran, Afghanistan, and beyond, Alexander did start to create settlements, usually named

Alexandria, including what is now Kandahar in Afghanistan. Plutarch, in his essay 'On the Virtue and Fortune of Alexander the Great', suggests that Alexander founded more than 70 cities, and claimed that his purpose in doing so was to spread Greek culture and learning among the 'barbarians'. The number is probably an exaggeration, but at least 20 settlements named Alexandria are known from inscriptions and written accounts. Not all of these have been securely located, and some, like Alexandria Troas near Troy, previously named Antigonia Troas after its founder Antigonus the One-Eyed, were given their name by later rulers. Some were refoundations of previously existing settlements, and others were new creations. Excavations at Ai-Khanoum in northeastern Afghanistan, which is thought to be the site of Alexandria-on-the-Oxus, have revealed a Greek theatre and temples, built some decades after Alexander's time, but Plutarch's idea that his foundations were intended as cultural centres is unrealistic. These settlements were mostly little more than fortresses, occupied by veteran Macedonian soldiers prepared to start a new life in Asia, supported perhaps by local inhabitants brought in from surrounding villages. These were not intended to be major commercial centres but points of control in regions where there was a danger of insurrection. When compared with all the other Alexandrias, the idea of Alexander deliberately created a new commercial city in Egypt seems out of place. It is possible that he might have wanted to leave a garrison fort there, and that this is what Ptolemy is referring to in the Satrap Stele, but the site of Alexandria is not an obvious one for a military settlement.

The stories of the omens surrounding the foundation of the city are above all reflections of its future success: the greater the fortune of the city, the more incentive there was to associate it with Alexander himself. Three of the early histories of Alexander had their origins in the city: Ptolemy, whose history is the main source for Arrian, Cleitarchus, whose work lies behind Diodorus and Curtius, and the so-called *Alexander Romance*, the fanciful popularizing account of Alexander's career that is known from versions from the 3rd century CE and afterwards, but which had its origins in the 3rd century BCE. Ptolemy in particular associated himself with Alexander, as we have seen, putting Alexander's head on his coins, and to credit Alexander with the founding of his royal city would assist him in this. Other authors would have no reason not to promulgate a version of the facts that raised the status of their own city. Older Greek cities claimed mythical heroes as their founders, and Alexander the Great was a hero worth claiming as founder by the Alexandrians, but the stories that Alexander did personally found the city belong more to legend than to history.

## The oracle of Amun

The Egyptian episode that receives the most attention in the surviving histories is Alexander's visit to the temple of Amun in the Siwa oasis in the Libyan desert. In addition to the accounts in Diodorus, Curtius, Plutarch, Arrian, and Justin, we have much of what Alexander's court historian Callisthenes wrote, as reported by the geographer Strabo, who wrote under the emperor Augustus, that is, a little later than Diodorus. Modern scholars have followed the ancient sources in seeing Alexander's encounter with the oracle as a turning point in his understanding of himself. As with other cases of Alexander's involvement with religion, however, the evidence is complex and confused.

The principal temple at Siwa was built in the reign of the pharaoh Amasis (570–526) for the god Amun, whose main centre of cult was at Thebes. At Thebes the oracle of Amun functioned in the traditional way of Egyptian oracles. At major festivals the image of the god would be carried in procession in his sacred boat, on the shoulders of eight priests. Those who wished to consult the god could ask their question as the god approached. If the god 'nodded' to them, that is if the cult image swayed towards them as it was being carried along, this would be taken as a positive answer, but if it swayed away from the enquirer it would indicate a negative response. Another method of questioning would be to place two alternative written statements along the path the god was travelling, and whichever of the two the god swayed towards would be taken to represent his decision. At Siwa the oracle operated in the same way. When Alexander visited the sanctuary the processional way led from the principal temple to a second smaller temple, built by Nectanebo II, and it was along this route that the cult image would have been carried. Since the oracle was in existence before the time of Nectanebo, his temple must have been constructed to increase the monumentality of the existing processional route.

From the time of the creation of the temple under Amasis, Siwa was visited by sacred ambassadors (*theoroi*) from the Greek city of Cyrene (near modern Benghazi), and Amun received cult in Cyrene under the name of Ammon or Zeus Ammon. He was depicted as a man with ram's horns, reflecting the Egyptian practice of representing Amun with a ram's head. Herodotus reports a consultation of the oracle by the Lydian king Croesus, which, if the report is accurate, would have taken place early in its history. Ammon was recognized in the Aegean in the 5th century, and in the early 4th century inscriptions indicate that the Athenians sent *theoroi* to the temple. But while the temple had some prestige in the Greek world, it was very much on the edge of Egyptian territory, and had far less prestige than Amun's much older temples in upper Egypt. It is unlikely therefore that Alexander visited it to impress the Egyptians, and the ancient writers do not describe the visit in those terms. It would make more sense to link Alexander's visit with his interest in establishing his authority over the Greek cities of Cyrenaica, which had come under Persian control in the time of Darius I, but had been left free from external control after the revolt of Egypt in 404.

Callisthenes claims that Alexander wanted to visit the oracle in emulation of his ancestors Perseus and Heracles, although there is no suggestion in earlier writers that these heroes did go to Siwa. Herodotus, who visited the oracle himself, and who tells stories of

Heracles' adventures in Egypt, tells how the hero went to visit the temple of his father Zeus at Thebes, and how Zeus, in order to prevent Heracles from seeing him as he was, wore a ram's head as disguise. But he says nothing about Heracles going to Siwa. Arrian, whose whole account appears based on Callisthenes (possibly by way of Ptolemy's history), gives the same explanation, but adds that Alexander wanted to find out about his *genesis*, that is his birth or his origins. Neither Callisthenes nor Arrian says what it was that Alexander asked the god. Of the other narratives only Justin offers an explanation of why he wanted to consult the oracle, elaborating the story that he wanted to know about his birth, but all four other authors do give a fuller account of Alexander's conversation with the priest—even if not a reliable one.

Ancient historians are often vague about the role of translators in encounters between foreigners. When Alexander visited Siwa it is unclear in what languages the various parties spoke. Plutarch, who several times in his *Life of Alexander* identifies linguistic jokes and puns, presents the Egyptian officials as speaking Greek, but doing so poorly: he suggests that the priest of Amun may accidentally have addressed Alexander as *Pai Dios* (Son of Zeus), because he was trying to say *paidion* (child). It would be, for Plutarch, a clever accidental omen, but none of the other writers describes the events in this way. They give the impression that all communication was direct, and could be interpreted in straightforward Greek terms. It is unlikely that Alexander understood Egyptian. It is possible that the priest of Amun understood Greek, since there was an established pattern of Greeks visiting the oracle. However, it is certain that Alexander will have been accompanied by interpreters, so that he will have known precisely what was being said. It is also likely that he will have been recognized as Pharaoh, or at least as the man soon to be crowned as Pharaoh, and therefore addressed with the formality that his office required.

This is significant because the ancient writers claim that when he first arrived at Siwa the priest of Amun addressed Alexander as son of the god (Diodorus), or specifically of Zeus (Callisthenes and Plutarch), Jupiter (Curtius), or Hammon (Justin). According to Diodorus, Curtius, and Justin, Alexander responded to this by saying that he would from this point on call himself by this title—suggesting that this was the beginning of a process that would end up by alienating Alexander from his men, because he was denying that Philip was his father. As we will see, however, Alexander's titles in Egypt, following Egyptian tradition, included the name 'Son of Re'; for him to be addressed as such by an Egyptian (or Libyan) priest will have been protocol, not revelation.

The more elaborate descriptions of Alexander's visit are generally thought to derive from the work of Cleitarchus, who was not an eyewitness to the visit, but, writing in Egypt, did understand how Egyptian oracles functioned: we are given slightly confused, but essentially authentic, descriptions of the statue being carried in its boat on the shoulders of the priests. But stories about the consultation of oracles in ancient historical narratives tend to conform to certain patterns, and the readers of the Alexander historians will have expected a spoken exchange between enquirer and priest, as was the pattern at the most famous Greek oracle, Delphi (although Delphi was notorious for the obscurity of its responses). The consultation of an oracle that responded solely by the movements of a statue would have been less easy to dramatize. As a result we are given a story that is not compatible with what we know about how Egyptian oracles functioned. Some scholars, including the excavators at Siwa, have attempted to reconcile the accounts by postulating a separate 'Royal Oracle' that was closer to the Greek model, but this is not compelling, and it makes more sense to allow the historians some dramatic licence in their retelling. These writers claim that Alexander asked two questions: whether his father's murderers had been punished and whether he would rule the world. The first of these seems designed in these accounts to reinforce the notion that Alexander had accepted divine paternity, as the oracle is said to have responded that his father could not be harmed by mortals (but that Philip's killers had been avenged). The second question received a positive response, and we will consider the implications of this later.

Stories about the consultation of oracles are common in Greek literature. The oracle of Delphi plays a major role in Herodotus' *History*, the first work of history to be written and one of the most influential. Oracular consultations feature prominently in many of Plutarch's *Lives*, and he wrote a series of essays about Greek oracles. It is therefore not surprising that the expedition to the oracle at Siwa is given a lot of attention in the narratives of the Greek and Roman Alexander historians. It demonstrated the involvement of the gods in Alexander's achievements, and revealed his greatness through the responses that the oracle gave. These confirmations of the nature of Alexander were important for the readers of those narratives, but the Egyptians themselves had other ways of making clear Alexander's significance and his relationship with the gods, above all by recognizing him as Pharaoh.

## Pharaoh Alexander

If we read the Greek and Roman histories with an understanding of what the Egyptians would have wanted from a new ruler, we can see that Alexander was able to live up to their expectations. Memphis, at the apex of the Nile Delta, the royal centre of Lower Egypt, was the administrative centre of Egypt in this period, and that is where Alexander went first. The normal rituals associated with the accession of a new pharaoh would start with the ceremonial proclamation of his royal names, and this would be followed by the pharaoh-to-be travelling to the major temples of the kingdom on a royal barge, a journey known as 'The Creation of Order in all Provinces'. All the kingdom's officials would be expected to renew their oaths of office, and foreign allies to renew their alliances at this time. The process ended with the coronation itself in Memphis, which would ideally take place at the time of the Egyptian New Year festival in June. None of the surviving authors actually describes Alexander's coronation, but they do refer to the occasions when the various rituals would have taken place. Arrian mentions two festivals at Memphis, one on Alexander's arrival and one shortly before his departure. Curtius says that from Memphis Alexander travelled up-river, presumably by boat, and he also reports a tragic incident when a young Macedonian noble drowned after the boat he was in capsized while it was attempting to catch up with Alexander. Arrian also describes Alexander receiving embassies and distributing offices while he was at Memphis before his departure.

The reluctance of the Greek and Roman authors to mention an actual coronation is significant. The same reluctance occurs in their accounts of Alexander's time in Babylon, where it is certain that he was enthroned as king, and at Susa, where it is highly likely. In part this may be a result of the authors' chosen narrative structure. They all, to a greater or lesser extent, present Alexander as being gradually corrupted by contact with the 'East': he is depicted as becoming increasingly interested in 'barbarian' practices and losing control over himself. This is a theme that we will consider elsewhere, but it is a storyline that would be weakened if Alexander were seen to be adopting the practices of the peoples he conquered too early in the journey.

Egypt had many temples, and work on restoring or extending them was one of the activities expected of a pharaoh. Two of the last native Egyptian rulers, Nectanebo I (380–362) and Nectanebo II (360–343), had been energetic in their building works, and it is likely that a number of works had been started by Nectanebo II but left unfinished when the Persians regained control of Egypt after its period of independence from them (404–343). Egyptian evidence indicates that Alexander was ready to follow in the tradition of temple-restoration.

At the great temple of Amun-Re at Luxor, near the ancient royal city of Upper Egypt, Thebes, Alexander is depicted on the walls of

**5. Alexander the Great (on the right) depicted as pharaoh in the temple of Amenhotep III at Luxor**

the 'chapel of the barque', which he is credited with restoring. In a sequence of reliefs in the traditional Egyptian style, Alexander is depicted dressed as pharaoh, facing the god Amun-Re. The accompanying texts identify him as 'King of Upper and Lower Egypt, Lord of the Two Lands, *Setepenre Meryamun* (Beloved of Amun, Chosen of Re), son of Re, possessor of the crowns, Alexander' (Figure 5). This is the standard form of address for a pharaoh, and the inscribed texts note that he has carried out the work for his father Amun-Re. The 'chapel of the barque' would have contained the cult image of the god, standing in a ceremonial boat. At major festivals the image would have been carried by the temple priests in procession in the boat. In the other great temple of Amun, nearby at Karnak, an inscription announces that Alexander had renovated the chapel of Tuthmosis III (Pharaoh 1475–1429) and once again Alexander is given his full pharaonic titles. Further downriver, at Hermopolis, inscriptions record further restoration work by Alexander. The picture we get from Egyptian monuments is of Alexander following in the footsteps of his predecessors, a picture significantly different, as we have seen, from that presented by the Greek and Roman accounts of his time in Egypt.

# Chapter 6
# King of the world: Alexander and Persia

The historian Appian, a contemporary of Arrian, reports a conversation between the Roman general, Scipio Africanus, and his tutor, the Greek historian Polybius, which took place outside Carthage in 146 BCE as that city was being sacked by the Roman army. Appian says that Polybius recorded the conversation as he heard it. Scipio, watching the destruction of the ancient city, was drawn to reflect on

> the inevitability that cities, nations and empires would be overthrown: such a fate had befallen Troy, a once fortunate city, and had befallen the Assyrians, the Medes and the Persians, whose empire had been greatest of all, and most recently the glittering empire of the Macedonians.

He went on to quote lines from the *Iliad*, where the Trojan prince Hector predicts the fall of Troy, and he explained to Polybius that he was thinking of the future time when Rome itself would fall.

The idea that different nations followed each other in ruling over large parts of the world, and in particular over Asia, was a well established theme in historiography by the time the surviving Alexander historians were writing. At the start of the last book of his *Anabasis* of Alexander, Arrian reports the unlikely suggestion that Alexander was planning to circumnavigate Africa and attack

Carthage from the west, and adds that in Alexander's view the Medes and Persians had no right to the title 'Great King' as they had only controlled the smallest part of Asia. This is probably a reflection of Arrian's own view rather than Alexander's, but Herodotus' account of the rise of the Persian empire, written a century before the reign of Alexander, presented the Persians as successor to the power of the Medes. Although 'rule over Asia' was not a precisely defined idea, it was what Alexander could expect to gain by defeating Darius, which he duly did for the second and final time at Gaugamela, near the modern city of Mosul in northern Iraq, on 1 October 331.

## 'King of the World'

We know the precise date of the battle of Gaugamela, and about some of the surrounding events, from a Babylonian astronomical diary like the example we met earlier in this book, noting Alexander's death. The Gaugamela diary, which covers the sixth and seventh months of the Babylonian year, equivalent to 8 September to 6 November 331, as all such diaries do, records each night's observations, and, if anything significant occurred, what rituals were carried out in response: on 25 September a dog was burned, possibly in response to a bolt of lightning (the tablet is broken at this point). At the end of the sixth month, *Ulūlu*, the tablet indicates how much barley, dates, mustard, cress, sesame, and wool could be bought in the market for a silver shekel; then which planets were in which constellations; and the height of the Euphrates. These data are followed by reports of other events, including an outbreak of panic in the camp of Darius on 18 September; the arrival of the Macedonian army at the battlefield; and the battle itself, during which Darius' troops, having been defeated, abandoned the king in their flight. This detail is of interest because it helps to resolve a disagreement amongst the Alexander historians: while Diodorus and Curtius claim that Darius held firm until after his troops began to flee, Plutarch and Arrian present Darius as the first to run. It is a case where the normally more reliable Arrian turns out probably to be incorrect.

The scribe who wrote out the tablet refers to Darius as 'the King', but to Alexander as 'King of the World'. There is some uncertainty about this translation, but similar titles are used to refer to Alexander in the surviving historians. Since the division of the world into continents was a creation of Greek geographers, Babylonians had no distinct concept of 'Asia', and 'King of the World' may have been a Babylonian way of rendering the term 'King of Asia'. Plutarch takes Alexander's victory at Gaugamela as the climax of his campaign, stating 'With the battle turning out this way, the rule of the Persians was considered to be completely overthrown, and Alexander, proclaimed as King of Asia, sacrificed to the gods on a grand scale and rewarded his friends with wealth, estates, and provinces.' This would be the situation the Babylonian scribe was responding to in his choice of title.

The title 'King of the World' first appears in the narrative of Alexander's campaigns in the story of the Gordian knot. At Gordium, the ancient capital of Phrygia, Alexander was shown a cart connected to a yoke by a complex knot, and was told that whoever could undo the knot would become either 'Ruler of Asia' (according to Arrian and Curtius) or 'King of the World' (according to Plutarch). Two versions of Alexander's response to this are reported—the more popular was that he simply cut the knot with his sword, but the alternative was that he pulled out a peg that held the knot together. In either case he was recognized as having fulfilled the prophecy. The versions of Alexander's consultation of the oracle at Siwa found in Plutarch, Diodorus, and Curtius (but not Arrian) also have Alexander being told that he will rule the world. There is no suggestion in these accounts that Alexander misunderstood the meaning of the oracle, or that it was unreliable. The responses can be understood as foretelling the outcome of Alexander's meeting with Darius, at Gaugamela, which followed his departure from Egypt.

## Susa

Defeated at Gaugamela, Darius III fled eastwards, and Alexander was able to lead his army south through Mesopotamia towards Persia. The first major city he came to was Babylon, and we will consider his relationship with that city later. From there he moved on to Susa, like Babylon an Achaemenid royal capital. Two of the Alexander historians report an odd story about Alexander's visit to the palace at Susa, which might be concealing an important event in Alexander's career. According to Diodorus and Curtius, Alexander went on a tour of the palace, and when he reached the throne room he sat on the royal throne. As he was not tall, Alexander's feet would not reach the floor in front of the throne, and so a page brought over a low table to serve as a footstool. At this one of the palace eunuchs began to wail, and eventually explained that this was the table at which Darius had formerly eaten his meals: the eunuch could not keep silent seeing this transformation of Darius' fortune. Alexander at first wanted the table removed, but his friend Philotas told him to treat the situation as an omen acknowledging Alexander's triumph.

What does the story tell us? It is unlikely to be true. Depictions of Achaemenid kings on their thrones generally show them with a footstool, and everything we know about 'the King's table' suggests that any table at which Darius dined would be unsuitable to act as a footstool. It is also unlikely that Alexander would have shown the kind of insensitivity the story implies. One possible interpretation of the episode is that it is a confused description of Alexander being enthroned and crowned as Great King. Plutarch, in his essay on *The Fortune of Alexander*, mentions an aged Greek called Demeratus weeping with happiness at the sight of Alexander sitting on the throne of Darius at Susa, and Susa was the usual place where Achaemenid kings were crowned. Plutarch, in his *Life of Artaxerxes*, describes his subject, Artaxerxes II, undergoing a different succession ritual, which took place at Pasargadae, but it is clear that Achaemenid kings performed different rituals in different places. The Alexander historians may have been uncomfortable describing Alexander willingly taking part in an Achaemenid ceremony, and thus retold the events as an omen-story, but we should not assume that Alexander shared their scruples.

This raises the question of what Alexander's ultimate aims were. Some historians have described Alexander as 'the last of the Achaemenids', suggesting that he saw himself as the successor to Darius III. On this view Alexander was planning to move the centre of his kingdom from Macedonia to the Achaemenid centres at Susa and Babylon. Associated with the move are his adoption of Persian dress and Persian court protocol, which are described as disturbing to his Macedonian companions. The alternative view would see these practices as necessary for the administration of the eastern parts of Alexander's empire, and would suggest that, had he lived longer, Alexander would have turned his attention westwards, and probably returned to Macedon.

To find our way through this uncertainty we have to start by thinking about the intended readers of the surviving narratives of Alexander's campaign. For the Roman readers of the histories of Alexander, the Persians were still the enemy. In place of the Achaemenid kings, the Romans faced the Parthian empire just across the Euphrates. Several Roman commanders had led expeditions across that river to take on the Parthians, with mixed results. Arrian had the emperor Hadrian in mind as a reader of his history, and Hadrian had campaigned with his predecessor Trajan in Armenia and Mesopotamia, and then, once he had become emperor, had withdrawn from the territories east of the Euphrates. Arrian tries to set Alexander up as a figure worthy of emulation by his Roman readers: he therefore plays down as far as possible any suggestions that Alexander might willingly have set himself up as Great King. But as we have seen, there is good reason to suppose that Macedonian court practices had always owed something to Persian models. Persian kingship will have appeared far less outlandish to Alexander and his Macedonians than it would have done to the Romans who read about him in the surviving accounts.

## The burning of Persepolis

Alexander understood the importance of gestures. He adopted Achaemenid protocols where it helped him maintain his authority, but his Achaemenid predecessors were prepared on occasions to demonstrate their power by destructive acts. One of the most notorious of Alexander's actions on his campaign was the burning of the palace of Persepolis. The palace had been built by Darius and Xerxes, the kings who had led armies into Greece, and the more popular story recorded in the surviving sources is that it was burnt down after a drunken party at which an Athenian courtesan, Thais, encouraged Alexander to take revenge for the destruction of Athens by Xerxes by destroying the palace that he had built. Versions of this story are told in all of the surviving accounts except that of Arrian, who reports that Alexander had the palace deliberately destroyed— an action Arrian himself appears not to have approved of. The material evidence tends to support Arrian's more sober view, and indicates that it was the contents of the palace as much as the building that were targeted (although the gold and silver were carried away first). The evidence of burning on the surviving stonework suggests that the furnishings had been piled up and set on fire.

Why Alexander should want to destroy Persepolis when he had done no damage to the other royal centres, Susa and Babylon, has puzzled scholars. It was not an act that would endear him to his new subjects, the Persians. The most likely explanation is that this was indeed a symbolic revenge for Xerxes' destruction of Athens. This was part of the justification for the participation of the Greek cities in the campaign, and it would have been difficult for Alexander to ignore it. He could rule his empire from the other royal centres, and did not need Persepolis. Later Persian tradition magnified the impact of the burning, claiming that along with the palace Alexander had destroyed the texts of ancient Zoroastrian religious works, but this is not plausible.

## Dressing as a Persian

For the Alexander historians, his campaign in Iran led to a relentless decline in Alexander's character, as he became increasingly drawn into 'eastern' forms of behaviour. They describe how he began to adopt Persian (or Median) forms of dress and court practices, including the mutilation of his opponents, and requiring his friends to prostrate themselves before him. At the same time they picture him becoming increasingly tyrannical: former friends were executed on trumped-up charges or murdered in violent rages. Modern scholars, while modifying elements of this narrative of corruption and decline, have tended to accept it as largely true. This is a mistake. Alexander's decline and fall was held up by moralists as the clearest example of seduction and corruption by the east. This reading of his life became the pattern for biographers and historians to use, but it obscures some important facts. Macedonian kings were part of a network that included the western Persian satraps, and many of the practices of satrapal courts, themselves influenced by the court of the Persian king, were adopted or adapted by the Macedonians and the other kings of the Aegean world: Alexander came to 'the east' familiar with its practices. We have also seen how in Egypt and Susa Alexander had no difficulty taking on the required role of pharaoh or king. The surviving narratives present Alexander gradually beginning to adopt Persian clothing, and later to 'experiment' with formal court protocol, facing the suspicion and even hostility of his fellow Macedonians in the process. But other stories, more favourable to Alexander, found particularly in Plutarch, depict his Macedonian friends sinking into luxurious living while Alexander set them an example of frugality and self-control. Neither version is convincing: both are more concerned with providing moral examples for the reader to emulate or resist than with accurately reporting what actually happened. It was the Roman writers and readers who might pretend to be shocked by Alexander's adoption of Persian dress in an Iranian climate, not his fellow Macedonians. So we may take it for granted that, from his time in Babylon and Susa onwards, if not earlier, Alexander's travelling court adopted protocols appropriate to the circumstances, and the king himself fully retained his intellectual capacity.

## Court ceremonial

The issue that most concerned the ancient writers, and many modern scholars, is the question of whether Alexander wanted his companions to prostrate themselves in his presence. The Alexander historians all appear to have believed that it was normal practice for Persians to prostrate themselves before the Great King, although this was not the case: only defeated enemies would have been required to do this. To make matters more complicated, the historians also suggested that prostration was a way of acknowledging the divinity of the Persian king. They report stories of how Alexander tried to introduce this practice into the protocol of his court, using social occasions as experiments and claiming that his achievements merited his being worshipped. In the stories, however, opposition to these changes is successfully led by Alexander's court historian, Callisthenes, and the practice is dropped.

Callisthenes, however, is an implausible leader of the resistance. His history of Alexander's campaign was notorious for its flattery. It was probably the source for the stories about Alexander's emulation of his heroic ancestors, Achilles, Heracles, and Perseus, and for depicting Alexander's expedition as a divinely ordained sequence of triumphs. In his description of Alexander's march along the south coast of Asia Minor he described the waves of the sea prostrating themselves before Alexander. Nor was Callisthenes himself popular: some stories told about him in the memoirs of Alexander's companions suggest that he was irritable and boorish at social occasions. But in 327 he was implicated in a plot against Alexander, was arrested, and died while under arrest. In the decades after his death he was reinvented as a principled opponent of Alexander's adoption of Persian practices and claims to divine descent. It is likely that the stories about the introduction of prostration, and Callisthenes' objection to it, were invented to make Callisthenes' death fit an established pattern of stories of philosophers standing up against tyrants. Encounters between philosophers and monarchs were a common subject for Greek writers, starting with Herodotus' account of the meeting of the Athenian philosopher-statesman Solon and Croesus, king of Lydia in the 6th century. Later history also had an influence: in the period shortly before Curtius, Plutarch, and Arrian were writing, the philosopher Seneca was ordered to commit suicide by the emperor Nero, whose tutor Seneca had been. So by the time the Alexander historians were writing, Callisthenes had become a philosophical martyr, killed for speaking truth to tyrannical power, and the stories about his opposition to prostration were too well known to be ignored. However, they are not compatible with what we know about Persian practices in Alexander's time and earlier, so they are not the best way of approaching the question of Alexander's interest in court ceremonial.

What we can say with more confidence is that Alexander appointed men to ceremonial positions that were a normal part of Achaemenid court life. He had a chamberlain or usher, a post known from Herodotus' description of palace organization under Darius I, where the usher controlled access to the king; his friend Hephaestion was given the title of *chiliarch*, another position that had been usual in the Persian court. He kept high ranking Persians in his entourage, including the son of his opponent Darius III, and when he distributed estates to his friends after the victory at Gaugamela, Alexander was acting like a Persian king, and effectively establishing these friends as the nobility of his new empire. Later in his reign, the descriptions of banquets that he organised for large numbers of leading Persians and Macedonians appear very similar to those known from earlier documents from Achaemenid Persepolis. The Alexander historians mention these facts in passing, and they do not suggest that they led to difficulties between Alexander and other Macedonians.

## Alexander's queens

Alexander's marriages demonstrate how he integrated himself into his new kingdom. As we have seen, his father Philip had several wives, and used marriage as a means of maintaining relationships with Macedon's neighbours. Persian kings bound powerful nobles to themselves in the same way, and especially in cases where the succession was not direct, they would marry former wives or daughters of their predecessors. As part of Alexander's settlement of the northeastern part of his empire, as we will see, he married Rhoxane, the daughter of a leading Iranian nobleman. On his return from the East in 324 he married two more women: Parysatis, the daughter of Artaxerxes III and sister of Artaxerxes IV, and Stateira, the daughter of Darius III. These marriages connected him to the families of the last two Persian kings, and, had Alexander lived longer, might have produced heirs to Alexander's throne who were direct descendants of his Achaemenid predecessors. Stateira and Parysatis had been captured by the Macedonians, along with the rest of Darius' household, in Damascus after the battle of Issus. The Alexander historians report that Alexander treated these captured women, who included Darius' wife and mother, with great respect. He might have married Stateira rather earlier than he did. All the Alexander historians mention letters sent by Darius to Alexander at times before the battle of Gaugamela, in which Darius offered him marriage to Stateira along with control of the territories west of the Euphrates. Such an agreement would effectively have made Alexander co-ruler with Darius, and presumably would have made it likely that a son of Alexander would inherit the whole empire eventually. Alexander's military triumph rendered this offer redundant, but a child of Stateira would have been a potential successor to Alexander. It is perhaps for this reason that Rhoxane, anxious to protect the status of her (as yet unborn) child, probably had Stateira and Parysatis killed not long after Alexander's death.

Discussion of Alexander's marriages inevitably leads to consideration of his attitude to sex more generally. This was a topic that ancient writers did not ignore, and which has interested modern scholars and influenced modern representations of Alexander. But the questions raised by the ancient writers were rather different from those which have been debated more recently. The Alexander historians do not give a great deal of detail about Alexander's sexual relationships, although Plutarch mentions briefly that he took as a mistress Barsine, the daughter of one of the leading Persians, Artabazus, and the widow of Darius' naval commander, Memnon of Rhodes, who was captured along with the rest of Darius' household after Issus. They are more interested in the issue of Alexander's self-control and sexual continence, as illustrated by his treatment of Darius' captured wife and daughters. Such continence was considered to be a particularly masculine virtue by ancient writers, who did not discuss sexuality in terms of sexual orientation. It is modern writers, including the novelists Klaus Mann and Mary Renault, and the film director Oliver Stone, who have drawn attention to the question of whether Alexander had sexual relations with men as well as women, drawing particular attention to Alexander's friendship with Hephaestion, and to stories about a Persian eunuch called Bagoas. While there is no explicit reference in the surviving texts to such relationships, they would not be inconceivable. There is, however, a danger that suggestions of Alexander's homosexuality romanticize him as much as references to his sexual continence, if they focus exclusively on consensual sexual relationships. Alexander spent most of his adult life on military campaigns and in a royal court where displays of power were a means of preserving order. Perhaps there should be debate, not on whether

Alexander ever had sex with another man, but on whether, or how often, he had sex by force with an unwilling partner, male or female. That kind of behaviour would have been beneath the notice of those who wrote about Alexander in his lifetime, but it has been a feature of all courts and all armies, so it would be truly remarkable if it was not part of Alexander's experience.

# Chapter 7
# Traveller: Alexander in Afghanistan and Pakistan

In the late Spring of 330 Alexander left Persepolis on a new campaign in the eastern parts of the empire he had won. It would be over five years before he returned. From the very start this journey to the east attracted more strange stories, and more moralizing commentary, than any other part of his career, and it has been a continuing source of fascination for historians in recent centuries. For ancient writers this was when Alexander was seduced by the luxuriousness of the east, and lost control of his passions. It was also when his unquenchable desire to go ever forward was eventually brought to a halt by his soldiers' refusal to go on. For modern writers Alexander's difficulty in dealing with insurgency in Afghanistan and the surrounding areas is the earliest evidence of the impossibility of governing that country; his killing of members of his court is presented as a sign that he was becoming a paranoid tyrant; and his treatment of the people of the Indus Valley is considered little short of genocide. Until recently there was little firm evidence to show what Alexander's eastern campaign involved, but the work of archaeologists, and the appearance and publication of documents from the Persian satrapy of Bactria, in what is now Afghanistan, offer some important correctives to the views of the ancient writers.

## Alexander and the queen of the Amazons

One episode in particular shows how early some fantastic stories were spread about Alexander's activities in the east. Curtius describes in some detail the visit of Thalestris, the Amazon queen, to Alexander's camp near the Caspian Sea. She was accompanied by 300 women warriors, and came with the intention of being impregnated by Alexander. To that end she spent 13 nights with the king before returning to her people. Plutarch provides details about where this story came from, saying that most of the authors he had read reported it, and naming five of them, but listing nine other authors who did not mention it. Both lists included men who had accompanied Alexander, but Plutarch tells a further story which casts doubt on the episode. Some years later, one historian, Onesicritus, was reading to Lysimachus, who had been one of Alexander's companions on the campaign: when he came to the story of the Amazon queen, Lysimachus is said to have smiled and asked, 'And where was I at the time?'

Curtius associated this story with Alexander's adoption of Persian dress and court practices, which he saw as a sign that Alexander had lost all self-control. Other historians also chose to wait until this point in the narrative to describe Alexander's adoption of Persian clothing, although, as we have seen, it is likely that the Macedonian court had been influenced by Persian protocol before Alexander's reign, and Alexander had already been acting in accordance with local expectations in Egypt, Babylon, and Susa.

## Into Afghanistan

Alexander's initial aim was to prevent Darius III from raising new forces in the eastern parts of his empire. However, by the summer of 330, Darius was dead, having been betrayed by his general Bessus, who declared himself king and took the throne-name Artaxerxes V. Alexander was then able to claim that, as the legitimate king, he was avenging Darius' death. His march took him through what is now northern Iran to Afghanistan, where he turned south to skirt the mountainous interior and then followed the route of the modern road from Kandahar to Kabul before turning northwest to Bactra (modern Balkh), and then across the Oxus River, which is now the border between Afghanistan and Uzbekistan, and in Alexander's time between the satrapies of Bactria and Sogdiana. By now Bessus had lost the trust of his fellow Persians, who turned on him and handed him over to Alexander. That was the Spring of 329, but there were another two years of fighting before Alexander was able to leave Sogdiana and Bactria: he faced insurgency in his rear and hostile neighbours on the other side of the River Tanais or Jaxartes.

The Greek and Roman narratives present the story of these years from the perspective of the Macedonian army and court. There are skirmishes fought and cities sacked, and from time to time troubles within Alexander's entourage. Little is said about those they were fighting against. As a result it is easy to imagine that Alexander was facing the same difficulties that the British had to deal with in the 19th century, the Russians in the 20th century, and NATO forces in the 21st. The historian George Grote, writing in the middle of the 19th century, referred to 'the rude, but spirited tribes of Baktria and Sogdiana', and the novelist Steven Pressfield depicted Alexander's infantrymen using the language, and sharing the attitudes, of contemporary US soldiers. But the region was no isolated wilderness in Alexander's time. Recently a number of documents dating from the reigns of Artaxerxes III and Alexander himself have revealed that it was very much integrated into the rest of the Persian empire.

These documents include letters written on leather, several of which were sent by Akhvamazda, who was probably the satrap of Bactria, to another official, Bagavant, in the period from 353 to 348. Akhvamazda has to deal with complaints about Bagavant's behaviour, and to make Bagavant get on with tasks set him. The

**6. A document from Bactria, written in Aramaic in 324, listing supplies being distributed in the satrapy**

responsibilities of both men extended to Sogdiana as well as Bactria. There are other letters and records of the distribution of supplies. Some of these records are very similar in form to documents recovered from Persepolis dating to the 5th century. All the Bactrian documents are written in Aramaic, which, by the 4th century, had become the language of administration throughout the empire (Figure 6). It is clear that Bactria, when Alexander arrived there, was a well organized region, integrated into the rest of the empire. The difficulties he faced in bringing the area under control were not that it was in the hands of quarrelling warlords, but that its administration could be effectively used by his opponents, in particular the rebel Spitamenes, who had turned Bessus over to Alexander, and then turned against him.

## The edge of empire

The northern boundary of Sogdiana, and of the Achaemenid empire, was the Jaxartes River, which was also known to the Greeks as the Tanais, and was recognized as dividing Asia from Europe.

83

Beyond lay Scythia, and Arrian and Curtius each have accounts of how Alexander crossed the river to take on the Scythians beyond. The two accounts are significantly different from each other, although each starts with Alexander sacrificing, with the intention of crossing the river, and receiving unfavourable omens. In Arrian's version, when a subsequent sacrifice also turns out unfavourably, Alexander decides to ignore the omens. He crosses the river and is initially successful, but then drinks some tainted water, falls seriously ill, and has to return across the river. In Curtius' story the second sacrifice is very positive; the bad omens turn out to have foretold an ambush of Alexander's men that had not yet been reported to Alexander, but the campaign across the Jaxartes is a complete success. Which of the two stories is correct is impossible to decide, but both suggest that the symbolic importance of Alexander crossing the Jaxartes was considerable.

Darius I had campaigned in the area in around 518, and in a later addition to the account of his reign he had inscribed at Behistun, he described how he crossed the 'sea' to fight the Scythians. Darius and his successors considered their empire to stretch from sea to sea, and in this conception the Jaxartes counted as a northern sea. In crossing the Jaxartes, but not attempting to hold on to the territory to its north, Alexander was following the practice of his Achaemenid predecessors in asserting the extent of his authority from sea to sea. And his later actions at the Hyphasis River in Pakistan were probably intended to achieve the same end.

Alexander was eventually able to settle affairs in Sogdiana and Bactria. As part of this process he followed an established Achaemenid practice of linking himself to the local Persian nobility by a marriage. His new wife was Rhoxane, daughter of Oxyartes, a leading Sogdian, whom Alexander later appointed as satrap of the area south of Bactria. The Greek and Roman historians appear unwilling to recognize Rhoxane's significance, suggesting that the marriage was a love-match, and in Curtius' case claiming that Rhoxane was socially far inferior to Alexander.

It is clear, however, that it was the marriage that consolidated Alexander's control of the region. One of the Bactrian documents discussed earlier is a long list of supplies which covers three months in year seven of Alexander's reign, that is 324: the satrapal administration was working smoothly then. In the following centuries Bactria was to become one of the most prosperous parts of what had been Alexander's empire.

## Court intrigues

Quite apart from the dangers of military activity, Alexander was at risk from attacks from within his court. The threats, such as they were, did not come from his close advisors, but on two occasions they had repercussions that led to the deaths of senior courtiers. For Alexander and his contemporaries, plots were an inevitable part of court life. His father had been assassinated by a former bodyguard, and it remained unclear whether that was part of a wider conspiracy. But for later writers, especially for those living under Roman emperors, these events were opportunities to consider how courtiers ought to behave in an autocracy. The dictatorships of the 20th century in turn provided models for modern scholars writing about Alexander's court, sometimes adding a further layer of anachronism to their accounts.

In the Autumn of 330 a conspiracy to assassinate Alexander involving a number of minor figures in his entourage was revealed. One of Alexander's companions, Philotas, son of Parmenion, was said either to have been implicated, or to have known about the plot, and done nothing to prevent it. Philotas was put on trial and condemned to death, and Alexander also ordered the death of Parmenion, who had been left in command in Ecbatana in Media. It is impossible at this distance to determine whether Philotas and Parmenion were guilty of anything, and it is likely that their deaths resulted from the inevitable rivalry between individuals of a royal court whose members were competing for the favour of the king. Arrian gives a brief account taking Philotas' guilt for granted. Curtius on the other hand provides a very elaborate description of Philotas' trial, complete with speeches of accusation on both sides. His version of events has some resemblance to accounts of trials of Roman senators under the emperor Tiberius, for which we have descriptions in the *Annals* of Tacitus. This was a way of bringing to life for his Roman readers the events of an earlier period when a ruler was becoming increasingly despotic and suspicious.

A second conspiracy led to another courtier's death. In Spring 327, around the time that Alexander married Rhoxane, a group of royal pages conspired to assassinate him. This followed the humiliation of one of the pages, named Hermolaus, during a hunt. The pages had easy access to the king, so were in a good position to carry out a plot against him, and this is what Hermolaus planned. It was only Alexander's staying up all night that saved him, and the next day the plot was discovered. In the investigation that followed, Callisthenes, Alexander's court historian, was implicated in the plot and arrested. As with other plots, we cannot know whether or not he was guilty, and in this particular case we do not even know what happened to him. Arrian says that the historians who were there at the time give conflicting accounts of his fate: Ptolemy said that he was executed, while Aristobulus stated that he died of disease while in custody. In the surviving narratives the real reason for the death of Callisthenes is taken to be his opposition to Alexander claiming divine status, and requiring his companions to prostrate themselves before him; the pages' plot merely provided the pretext for his arrest. Most modern scholars have accepted this version of events, but, as we have seen, it has its problems.

One other significant death of a courtier occurred between the arrests of Philotas and Callisthenes: Alexander ran his companion Cleitus through with a spear after a drunken dinner. Cleitus was a cavalry commander under Alexander's father Philip, and had kept that role under Alexander. He was said to have saved Alexander's life at the Battle of the Granicus in 334. In the autumn of 328 Alexander appointed him satrap of Bactria. At a dinner soon after this, according to all the surviving narratives, an argument broke out between the two men. Accounts of the substance of the argument, and of what the protagonists actually did, are inconsistent and probably unreliable, but the evening ended with Alexander killing Cleitus. Both men were probably drunk. Roman moralists drew parallels between the deaths of Cleitus and Callisthenes, as two examples of the king killing his friends, and the authors of the surviving narratives put similar accusations into the mouths of both men—in particular that Alexander was dishonouring the memory of his father Philip by claiming to be son of Zeus. This was a standard accusation made against Alexander in later periods, and gave greater significance to Cleitus' death as being one more example of a death resulting from Alexander's increasing loss of awareness of his own mortality. But in all likelihood it was the proximity of men, alcohol, and weapons in the atmosphere of rivalry and ambition that would characterize any royal court that best explains what happened.

## To the Indus Valley

From Afghanistan Alexander marched southeast through the Hindu Kush and into the northern part of the Indus River basin in what is now Pakistan. According to Herodotus' *Histories*, Darius I had campaigned in this region, and the parts of what he calls India west of the Indus paid tribute to the Persian king. Not a lot is known about the region between the time of Darius I and Alexander, so it is not clear how far to the east the authority of the later Achaemenid kings reached, although Arrian says that a contingent of the Indians who bordered Bactria fought alongside the Bactrians at the battle of Gaugamela. For the Greek and Roman historians, this was not a significant issue in any case. Their narratives focus more on the idea of Alexander travelling further east than his heroic predecessors had gone. Alexander captured a supposedly impregnable fortress, the Rock of Aornus, which even Heracles was said to have been unable to storm, and he and his companions spent time in the city of Nysa, once visited by Dionysus, as was proved by the presence there of ivy, a plant particularly associated with the god, which was apparently found nowhere else in the region.

Four major tributaries flow into the Indus from the east, coming down from the Himalayas: from west to east, the Hydaspes (modern Jhelum), Acesines (Chenab), Hydraotes (Ravi), and Hyphasis (Beas). The territory between these rivers was controlled by a number of rival Indian princes. Alexander adopted a different pattern of control here from other parts of the empire. He did not appoint satraps and local military commanders, but rather he confirmed in their positions those princes who agreed to accept his authority. The first significant ruler to do this was Taxiles, whose territory lay between the Indus and the Hydaspes. Consequently Alexander was faced with opposition from Taxiles' neighbour Porus, on the east side of the Hydaspes.

Alexander's defeat of Porus, which followed his rapid crossing of the river, was the fourth and last major pitched battle of the campaign in Asia. A series of large silver coins, or medallions, were struck to commemorate the victory. Known as Porus decadrachms or Elephant medallions, these depict on one side a lone horseman attacking an elephant with two tall riders, one of whom is throwing a spear at the horseman—generally assumed to be a depiction of Alexander and Porus—and on the other side Alexander himself in full armour, holding a thunderbolt and being crowned with a wreath by a winged victory (Figure 7). These attributes should probably be associated with the title of 'unconquered god' that the Athenians were to bestow on Alexander some two years later on his return from this campaign. The coins or medallions were probably issued to Alexander's soldiers as a reward for their service. They show Alexander as his troops would want to imagine him, all-powerful

7. A coin or medallion issued by Alexander to celebrate victory in his Indian campaign. The obverse shows a horseman attacking an elephant with a warrior on its back, probably representing Alexander and Porus. The reverse shows Alexander, in armour, holding a thunderbolt and being crowned by Victory

and victorious, and the Greek cities would have recognized his success in similar terms. But the coins should not be seen as Alexander making claims himself for any 'divine status'.

Alexander's treatment of Porus after the battle became a popular subject, not least in a series of operas using a libretto by the 18th-century Italian poet Metastasio, and in the first full-length movie about Alexander, Sorab Modi's *Sikandar* of 1941. Porus pledged allegiance to Alexander, who restored him to his position, and even increased the size of his territories.

## Turning back?

After this Alexander continued eastwards over the Acesines and Hydraotes as far as the Hyphasis, which became the scene of one of the most frequently told stories about Alexander. It was on the banks of the Hyphasis, according to tradition, that Alexander's soldiers finally refused to accompany him any further. In response Alexander supposedly shut himself up in his tent and refused to see anyone, and then said that he would go on alone. But when even this would not make his soldiers change their minds, he submitted to their will and turned back. This is one of the stories found in all the surviving narratives, and as a result its veracity has seldom been doubted, but all that this unanimity really proves is that the story had come into circulation before the earliest of the surviving narratives had been composed: it was so memorable a story that no subsequent narrator could ignore it. There is good reason to suppose that the story is an invention. Before he marched east from the Hydaspes, Alexander had commissioned the building of a fleet of transport ships to take his army down-river. It is likely that the Hyphasis was considered the boundary of the Persian empire towards India, just as the Jaxartes was north of Sogdiana. It may have been the case that Alexander had intended to cross the Hyphasis to assert his authority, and then return to its west bank, just as he had done both at the Jaxartes and also at the Danube at the start of his reign. If so, then according to Ptolemy, as reported by Arrian, it was unfavourable omens rather than Alexander's soldiers that prevented him. Alexander's activities in the eastern part of the empire make more sense as the consolidation of his rule over the territory he had won from Darius III, rather than an endless quest for new conquests. The authors of the Alexander histories had no interest in where the existing boundaries of the Achaemenid empire lay, so they present Alexander's every move as winning new territory, but Alexander himself will have known better. Having reached the eastern edge of the territories he had already laid claim to, he was ready to turn south and march towards the ocean. He was not turning back homewards yet.

## To the ocean

For the story of Alexander's journey through the Indus Valley to the Indian Ocean we are entirely reliant on the Alexander historians. No inscriptions from Greeks or Indians have survived, and the constantly changing courses of the major rivers have erased any archaeological remains that there might have been.

Alexander sailed down the Hydaspes while contingents of his army marched alongside on either bank. His aim appears to have been to assert his authority by confirming those local leaders who acknowledged his sovereignty in their positions, and campaigning vigorously against those who resisted him. This was no different from his policy elsewhere, but modern scholars have tended to present this phase of the campaign as particularly violent and destructive. Certainly Alexander did face resistance in some places, and he received his most severe wound during the siege of a city somewhere in the southern Punjab. South of Punjab, although his army marched, and where necessary fought, through the territory on the eastern side of the Indus, Alexander was not concerned to establish direct rule over that territory, and he probably followed Darius I in treating the river as the eastern boundary of his empire. As it turned out, this was one of the first parts of Alexander's empire to be taken over by others. Plutarch reports a visit by a young Indian prince (whom he calls Androcottus) to the court of Alexander when he was in the Punjab. That prince was Chandragupta Maurya, who came to power in around 322, and rapidly gained control of most of northern India from the Ganges Delta to the Indus. By the time he abdicated in 290, the Mauryan empire included most of South Asia, including the satrapies along the west bank of the Indus.

For Alexander it is clear that his arrival at the Indian Ocean marked the successful end of his campaign, and this was celebrated by sacrifices to the gods made out at sea. But the final stage of his campaign was to become the most notorious of all his travels, and possibly the most misunderstood.

## The Gedrosian Desert

Alexander had brought a fleet down from the Punjab to the Indian Ocean, and his intention was to send it on up the Persian Gulf to the mouths of the Tigris and Euphrates, and from there upriver to Babylon. To have a naval route that reached from Mesopotamia almost to Afghanistan would have been of great value, but it relied on the fleet being supplied as it sailed along the largely inhospitable south coast of Iran. It was for this reason that Alexander led a land force through the region of Gedrosia in southern Iran on his way from the Indus Delta back to Pasargadae. His purpose, as Arrian describes it, was to make sure that there was fresh water and supplies of grain available to the fleet as it sailed up the gulf. There is no doubt that this was a difficult task, as the territory was mostly desert and there were few good anchorages at the coast. The land expedition took two months, but it should be judged a success, as the fleet, under the Cretan commander Nearchus, was able to complete its journey without difficulty.

Ancient authors writing after Alexander's time transformed the march through Gedrosia into a disaster resulting from Alexander's arrogance and folly. After a sober account of how, with some difficulties, Alexander was able to achieve his aim, Arrian reports a series of stories about the hardship of the desert journey that he did not find in his main sources, but must have considered 'worth telling and not entirely implausible'. Plutarch claims that he lost three-quarters of the army he took to India in the Gedrosian desert, even though he took far fewer than half of his troops into Gedrosia. Modern scholars have perhaps been too ready to believe the horror stories, even suggesting that the march through the desert was Alexander's way of taking revenge on his soldiers for forcing him to turn back at the Hyphasis. This was not what the ancient writers thought. Arrian reports the view that Alexander was seeking to outdo his famous predecessors, Cyrus the Great and Semiramis, the legendary queen of Babylon, each of whom had gone through the desert and lost almost their entire army. We should recognize in the stories of the desert journey an interest not in Alexander's folly, but in his superhuman endurance.

Once he had led his army out of the desert, the road was open first to Pasargadae and Persepolis, and then to Susa and Ecbatana, before the final chapter in Alexander's life opened on the road to Babylon.

# Chapter 8

# Doomed to die: Alexander in Babylon

The final chapter of Alexander's life was set in Babylon. He had spent a short time there earlier in his campaign, and it had been the first Achaemenid royal centre that he had visited. We have already come across the fragment of a Babylonian astronomical diary that reports Alexander's victory at the battle of Gaugamela, and refers to him as 'King of the World'. That diary goes on to report his negotiations with the governor of Babylon, his promise to restore Esagila, the sanctuary of the god Marduk, and his entry into the city of Babylon itself on 20 October 331. Alexander was to return to Babylon nearly eight years later, in Spring 323, and it was there that he died. Babylonian documents can illuminate important aspects of Alexander's actions in the city and his relationship with its scholar-priests. They can also help us make sense of some puzzling stories in the Greek and Roman accounts.

## Babylonian scholarship

The scholars who produced the astronomical diaries were also responsible for composing the Babylonian royal chronicles. Like the diaries these record significant historical events, without commenting upon them, and they therefore differ from the royal inscriptions, which were designed for public consumption and which emphasize the virtues and power of the king. The sequence of chronicles starts at the accession of king Nabonassar (747–734), and is known to carry on at least into the later 2nd century BCE. The eight years during which Alexander was king, though they were important in Babylonian history, are only a brief moment in this context.

As well as making records of the present, the Babylonian scholars also created works of guidance based on past events. These included the *Enūma Anu Enlil*, which listed celestial events, in particular eclipses, with guidance as to what they portended. The aim of all this was to support the king, so that his reign would be long and the city of Babylon would benefit from it. So as well as recording celestial events and identifying potential threats to the king, the scholar-priests would advise him on what actions to take to avoid the predicted dangers.

## Alexander's entry into Babylon, 331

When Alexander entered Babylon after his victory at Gaugamela, he was following in a line of previous victorious new rulers that included Sargon II of Assyria (722–705) and Cyrus the Great of Persia. The account of Alexander's entry into Babylon recorded by Curtius follows a pattern known from official documents produced by these earlier kings. The people of the city are described as rejoicing, and the new king in turn sacrifices to the gods and promises to restore their temples. The promise to restore the temples did not necessarily indicate that they had been damaged earlier: large brick-built buildings were in need of constant attention, and kings could improve them as well as keep them standing: the king's concern for the fabric of the city was a sign of his virtue. Arrian claims that Xerxes had destroyed the temples of Babylon, but there is no mention of this in any Babylonian documents.

None of the surviving narratives mentions a coronation of Alexander in Babylon, but he was certainly recognized as king from the time of his arrival, and described as such in Babylonian documents from this time and afterwards. For Plutarch, the fact that Alexander was prepared to surround himself with Babylonian soothsayers was a sign that he was becoming enmeshed in superstitious practices, but it was an inevitable consequence of his position as king that the religious-administrative organization of the city would be deployed to advise and support him. He did not stay long in Babylon on this occasion, moving on to the other Persian royal centres at Susa and Persepolis. But Alexander was to return to Babylon at the end of his life, and once again he would follow the guidance of its priests.

On 20 September 331, the 13th day of the month *Ulūlu* in the Babylonian calendar, 11 days before the battle of Gaugamela, there had been a lunar eclipse. Saturn was in the sky, and Jupiter had set. This is recorded in the astronomical diary already discussed, and the eclipse is mentioned by the surviving Alexander historians. In the *Enūma Anu Enlil* there is an explanation of the meaning of an eclipse on that day. Not only does it foretell the death of the current king, but also that his son will not inherit his throne, and a new ruler will come from the west and rule for eight years. The battle that followed the eclipse in September 331 did indeed ensure the end of Darius' reign, and sometime after that of his life. He was indeed succeeded by a ruler from the west, Alexander. But October 323 would mark the end of eight years of Alexander's reign. Unless fate could be avoided, Alexander's future was looking bleak.

## Alexander's entry into Babylon, 323

Alexander had returned from his Indian campaign at the end of 325. After spending the summer of the following year in Ecbatana in Media, and campaigning against the Cossaeans in the northern Zagros Mountains in the autumn and winter, Alexander made his way to Babylon in the spring of 323. There, according to Arrian and Diodorus, he was discouraged from entering the city by the

Babylonian priests, on the grounds that it would be dangerous for him. Possibly they were influenced by two eclipses, one lunar, one solar, that had occurred the previous May. The meaning of the lunar eclipse on that particular day was that 'the King of the World would die and his dynasty would come to an end'. Such predictions were supposed to come true within 100 days, but occasionally came into effect later. It is also likely that the priests were expecting solar eclipses in April and May 323, although these turned out not to be visible. Arrian says Alexander was advised not to enter the city from the west, and he adds that according to Aristobulus, who was with Alexander at the time, the king attempted to follow this advice, but was prevented from getting round the city because the ground was waterlogged and marshy. It is common in narratives involving prophecies of misfortune that the central character tries to avoid ill luck, but is prevented by circumstances beyond his control, and Arrian is clearly conscious that this is the message of this story, but that does not mean that it is not a basically accurate account.

It seems likely that, either after Alexander had entered Babylon against advice, or while he was waiting to enter the city, another ritual was performed to protect him from ill fate. This was the 'substitute king ritual', which is known from Assyrian texts. The ritual involved the temporary abdication of the king, usually for 100 days, with a criminal or madman being made king in his place. The idea was that any misfortune would fall on the substitute instead of the real king. Once the predicted risk period was over, the substitute would be executed, and the real king would resume his reign. There are no Babylonian documents that refer to this ritual, but the Greek writer Dio Chrysostom, a contemporary of Plutarch, makes a confused reference to it as a Persian custom. It was probably taken over by the Babylonians from the Assyrians, and used by them into the Persian period and beyond. In the narratives of Diodorus, Plutarch, and Arrian, stories are told about a madman or lunatic being found sitting on the throne, wearing Alexander's royal gown and diadem. In the stories this is presented as an omen of Alexander's impending death, and it is suggested that the man went to the throne of his own accord. However, the similarities to the elements of the substitute king ritual are too close to be coincidental, so they may be taken as evidence for Alexander undergoing such a ritual in 323. However, he was clearly back on the throne by June.

## Death

Plutarch and Arrian both give quite detailed accounts of the last days of Alexander's life. They based these on what they believed to be genuine reports of his daily activities recorded in the so-called 'Royal Journals'. While it is not unlikely that such records might have existed, most scholars doubt that what was available to writers of the 2nd century CE bore much of a relationship to them. Following the account in these journals, Plutarch and Arrian describe how Alexander caught a fever and spent the last few days of his life mainly lying on his couch, conducting the religious rituals required of him as king and giving instructions to his officers about a planned invasion of Arabia. He gradually weakened, and sometime before he died he lost the ability to speak. None of this is implausible. Although Alexander was only 32 years old, he had suffered a number of injuries, including a severe chest wound in the Punjab. He also drank alcohol heavily. His companion Hephaestion had died under similar circumstances in Ecbatana the previous year, with no foul play suspected.

Inevitably, however, within a few years of his death, stories began to circulate that claimed that Alexander had been poisoned. The version we find in most of the Alexander historians claims that Alexander's regent in Greece, Antipater, organized the assassination, sending his sons Cassander and Iollas to Babylon with poison provided by Aristotle. It is most likely that this story was invented to damage the reputation of Antipater and Cassander in the conflicts between Alexander's successors that broke out immediately after his death. Alexander's mother, Olympias, working in the interest of her grandson, Rhoxane's infant son Alexander IV, found herself in opposition to Antipater and Cassander and may have been the source of the story.

The most widespread story about Alexander's death, however, concerns his supposed last words. Arrian reports, on the basis of the supposed 'Royal Journals', that Alexander lost the power of speech a few days before he died, but, because the story was too well known to be ignored, he also notes that some writers said that Alexander's companions asked him to whom he left his kingdom, and that Alexander's reply was 'to the strongest'. The events of the years following Alexander's death made such a response seem prophetic. Alexander's generals fought among themselves over the next decades, attempting either to take control of his whole empire or, eventually, to carve out kingdoms for themselves. Even when he was dead, Alexander was still a part of this conflict. As we have seen, his body, which was being sent back to Macedonia to be buried in the royal tombs at Vergina, was diverted to Egypt, where Ptolemy, who made himself first satrap and later pharaoh in Egypt, used it to legitimize his rule.

The empire which Alexander had created began to fall apart even before his body had been properly buried. There is no space in a book of this size to tell the story of the following years, which has in any case been told often before. What remains is to look at how the historical Alexander, whom we have glimpsed through the fragmentary contemporary evidence, and through the distorting lens of later historical tradition, reached the position he occupies in the imagination of the modern world.

# Chapter 9
# After Alexander

This book has tried to show what we can say with confidence about
Alexander and his world, on the basis of evidence from his own
time. Often this has meant challenging commonly held ideas about
how he acted, why he did what he did, and even questioning
whether he did do some of things attributed to him. But if long-held
ideas about Alexander are unreliable or wrong, where did they
come from in the first place? In this last chapter we will look at
Alexander's afterlife, and how some of the images of Alexander that
are prominent in popular imagination came into existence.

## Roman Alexanders: Julius Caesar and others

In 45 BCE the Roman Senate voted to put up in the Temple of
Quirinus in Rome a statue of Julius Caesar, with the title *Deus
Invictus* ('The invincible god'). Caesar, who was to be assassinated
the following year, at this point held the position of dictator, with
what amounted to absolute political power in Rome. The title
*Deus Invictus* (Greek *Theos Aniketos*) was identical to that the
Athenians had given to the statue of Alexander they voted in 324,
ironically also the year before his death. It is unlikely that the
choice of title was coincidence. At the time that the statue was
voted on, the leading politician (and part-time philosopher)
Cicero was attempting to compose a letter of advice to Caesar on

how to rule, in deliberate imitation of a letter supposedly written to Alexander by his former tutor, Aristotle. In the end Cicero abandoned the idea, noting in a letter to his friend Atticus that 'even Aristotle's pupil, whose temperament and self-control were of the best, became proud, cruel and intemperate once he was addressed as king'. It suited the moralists of the Roman republic, which had an ideology of opposition to monarchy, to see Alexander's taking of Darius' throne as the beginning of a decline into tyranny.

Parallels between Julius Caesar and Alexander, the two greatest military figures of their ages, were readily drawn. Plutarch's *Life of Alexander* is paired with his *Life of Julius Caesar*, and several writers tell a story of how Caesar, in Spain, before his career had taken off, saw a statue of Alexander and wept at how little he had achieved by the age at which Alexander had died. He was not the only Roman to see Alexander as a potential model. His older contemporary and rival Pompey, who had annexed the territories of the eastern Mediterranean, which had formerly been part of Alexander's empire, for Rome, adopted the cognomen Magnus, 'the Great', and modelled the hairstyle of his portrait statues on that of Alexander. So Alexander could provide a model for ambitious individuals. The man who commissioned the Alexander Mosaic in Pompeii (see Figure 1 in the Introduction) around the time of Pompey's birth presumably also saw Alexander as a figure worthy of being depicted in the more public area of his home. The implication might be that visitors would associate Alexander's virtues with his own.

On 15 February 44, at the festival of the Lupercalia, Caesar's lieutenant Mark Antony offered a diadem to him, which Caesar declined. It was suspected by some contemporaries that Caesar had arranged the event as a way of claiming the title of king, as if by popular demand; others interpreted his action, placing the diadem on a throne next to him, as making a claim for worship as a god, since gods were regularly represented in Roman processions by attributes carried on thrones. It is probable that these two interpretations could have been held together. Kingship, in this period, was considered a characteristic of the Persian and Hellenistic east, and Romans were under the impression that in that part of the world, kings were worshipped as gods. Whatever precisely happened, this diadem incident has been seen as a trigger for Caesar's assassination exactly a month later by men claiming to be defending the republic. It was in the years after this assassination that the earliest of our surviving narratives of Alexander's life, Book 17 of Diodorus' *Library of History*, was written, and memories of Caesar's life and death must have influenced the way he and his readers will have interpreted the life of Alexander. It will also have influenced Diodorus' contemporary, Pompeius Trogus, whose history survives now in an epitome, an abbreviated version made around 300 years later by Justin.

Julius Caesar had come to power during the period of political chaos and civil war which led to the collapse of the Roman republic. His adopted son, who took the name Augustus, brought an end to the wars and, while claiming to be restoring rule to the senate and people of Rome, established himself as the first Roman emperor. For Augustus and his successors, the question of how to reconcile the need for a single leader with the Roman tradition of republican rule was an on-going concern, and this is an underlying theme in the stories we find in the narratives of Tacitus and Suetonius, who were writing at about the same time as Plutarch and Arrian, and of Cassius Dio, writing in the early 3rd century CE. Some emperors are portrayed as less successful than others, in particular Caligula, who became emperor in 37 CE. Caligula is said to have taken Alexander the Great's breastplate to wear when, like Julius Caesar and Augustus before him, he visited Alexander's tomb in Alexandria. He is also said to have required Roman senators to prostrate themselves in front of him, offering them his toe to kiss instead of his hand. Curtius' generally negative depiction of Alexander may have been influenced in part by memories and representations of Caligula: Curtius was writing either in the reign of Caligula's successor Claudius, or under Vespasian a few decades later.

By the time Plutarch and Arrian were writing, under the successful emperors Trajan (98–117) and Hadrian (117–38), it was accepted that the Roman Empire was an autocracy. Alexander came to be presented as a model of correct kingship: these writers emphasized his wisdom and self-control while warning of the potential dangers of adopting the habits of eastern rulers. Both emperors led armies across the Euphrates into Mesopotamia, following in the footsteps of Alexander, so it was appropriate for contemporary writers to present him as both a symbol of military success and a warning about the dangers of luxury and excess.

The Alexander that has come down to us in the ancient historical narratives grew under particular circumstances. He is the creation of Roman authors (even if several of them wrote in Greek), writing for a Roman audience. Roman concerns, about how to be a ruler, and how to live as a subject under an autocracy, which are central themes in Roman histories of Rome, are equally present in histories of Alexander the Great, as is a suspicion and hostility of their eastern neighbours. In more recent times these concerns have sometimes arisen again: the period of dictatorship in Europe in the second quarter of the 20th century, and the rebirth of the idea of the 'clash of civilizations' in the wake of 9/11 have both had their impact on Alexander studies, as the prejudices of the Romans have seemed to pre-echo the politics of the 20th and 21st centuries.

## Medieval Alexander

If we want to know about Alexander today, it is to the Alexander historians of the Roman period that we turn for our information. However, for most of the period between Alexander's death and the present there was another tradition of stories that was much more prominent. In his *Monk's Tale* Chaucer gives a brief account of Alexander's career and comments that:

> The storie of Alisaundre is so commune
> That every wight that hath discrecioun
> Hath herd somwhat or al of his fortune.

The story that the Monk is referring to is known as the *Alexander Romance*, an account of Alexander's life that had its origins in Egypt in the 3rd century BCE, and was developed over the following centuries, translated into numerous languages, until versions of it were known from Iceland to India.

The earliest version of the *Alexander Romance* that we can read comes from the 3rd century CE. It tells the story of Alexander's life, with fanciful elements that became even more exaggerated in later versions. Alexander is said to be the son of the last Egyptian pharaoh, Nectanebo, who is also a magician, and who comes to Philip's court and seduces Olympias by disguising himself as the god Ammon in the form of a serpent. Nectanebo acts as Alexander's first tutor, but Alexander kills him when he reveals himself to be his father. In later Persian tradition, as recorded in the *Shahnameh*, or *Book of Kings*, written around 1000 CE, Alexander has become Sekandar, supposedly son of Philip, but actually the son of Darab, king of Persia, and therefore half-brother of his opponent Dara (Darius III). These alternative filiations tie Alexander more firmly to the kingdoms he comes to rule. Other elements of his early life are made more fantastical: for example in the *Romance* his favourite horse, Bucephalas, is depicted as not just untameable by anyone but Alexander, but also as a man-eater. Another story tells of the young Alexander going in disguise to spy out the court of the Persian king before he begins his campaign. In versions of the story told after the Arab conquests of the 7th century CE, Alexander is said to have gone in disguise to the royal court of Islamic Andalusia, where the queen immediately sees through his disguise.

Many of the events recorded in the more sober accounts of Alexander's career are also described in the *Romance*, although not in the same order. In particular Alexander's siege of Tyre is described with considerable detail. Later versions of the *Romance* include more miraculous tales: Alexander is taken up into the sky in a chariot drawn by griffons, and goes down to the depths of the sea in a glass diving bell; he visits paradise and has his own death foretold. Over time the story told in the *Romance* tells more and more about Alexander's search for wisdom, and in the versions written down in medieval western Europe Alexander becomes a symbol of chivalry and goodness.

It is through this *Romance* tradition that Alexander, under the name *o Megalexandros*, continued to be known in Greece through centuries when knowledge of classical history and mythology was lost. An early modern Greek version of the *Romance*, the *Phyllada*, or *Book of Alexander the Great*, was published in Venice in 1670, and remained in circulation continuously from then onwards. Alexander also became, uniquely among figures from classical antiquity, a character in a number of Karagiozis shadow-puppet plays. This form of popular entertainment grew out of an Ottoman Turkish tradition, developing its Greek character through the 19th century, and reaching the peak of its popularity in the first half of the 20th. *O Megalexandros* appeared in several plays, most notably in 'Alexander the Great and the Cursed Snake', in which, in keeping with the development of his character into that of a brave warrior righting wrongs, he kills a dragon which is terrorizing a kingdom: he has become a version of St George.

The presence of Alexander in Greek popular culture in the role of a largely Christianized warrior hero may be part of the explanation for the strength of the reaction in modern Greece to the deployment of the image of Alexander. This has been a particular issue in the relationship between Greece and the (former Yugoslav) Republic of Macedonia, where the decision in 2006 to name the airport at Skopje after Alexander the Great, and to erect a huge equestrian statue of him on the site, led to protests from the Greek government.

## Alexander, the Enlightenment, and empire

The chivalrous Alexander of the *Romance* suited the medieval world, and the courts of the absolutist monarchs like Louis XIV and Catherine the Great. New Alexanders emerged in the Age of the Enlightenment, the period from the late 17th until the early 19th century. Initially in France, but then in Scotland and England, and eventually Germany and elsewhere, *philosophes* and historians brought a more critical approach to the study of ancient history and of Alexander the Great in particular. New editions and translations were made of the Greek and Latin Alexander historians, and their reliability was held up to scrutiny. At the same time Alexander was reconsidered as model ruler. Some writers chose to stress his negative characteristics, his cruelty, and, not least, his persecution of scholars like the court historian Callisthenes. But this was a period of European expansion overseas, and for others Alexander's campaigns were seen as bringing the benefits of a lively and progressive European civilization to the slothful and unchanging east. For such writers there was effectively no difference between the empire of Darius III and the Ottoman Empire of their own time. The most positive assessments of Alexander can be found in a number of essays by Voltaire and in the treatise on *The Spirit of the Laws* by the Baron de Montesquieu: they suggest that Alexander's greatest achievement was to open up the east to trade and commerce, through his city-foundations, and the naval voyages he organized.

For writers in England and Scotland, the loss of Britain's American colonies in the War of Independence was the impetus for renewed study of ancient Greek history. In 1786 the Scottish historian John Gillies published a two-volume *History of Ancient Greece, its Colonies and Conquests*. Dedicated to the king, George III, it was written in reaction to the events in America with the explicit intent of demonstrating the dangers of democracy or republicanism and the superiority of constitutional monarchy. Two years earlier the English Conservative MP William Mitford had published the first volume of his eight-volume *History of Greece*. By the time he published his last volume, the French Revolution had taken place, offering an even clearer lesson about the dangers of the unrestrained rule of the people. For Gillies and Mitford democratic Athens, defeated in the 5th century by monarchic Sparta and in the 4th by the Macedonians under king Philip, represented all that was wrong with democracy, and in contrast the career of Alexander was the best example of what monarchy could achieve. For Gillies, Alexander was 'this extraordinary man, whose genius might have changed and improved the state of the ancient world'.

Alexander's 'civilizing mission' was a theme that was used to justify British involvement in India, which after the loss of the American territories became the main focus for colonial expansion. Following the example of earlier French writers, advocates of imperialism depicted the British as Alexander's heirs, bringing European energy and civilization to Asia, sunk in lethargy. But Alexander's legacy could be claimed by others too. Sir Alexander Burnes, who was British political agent in Kabul before he was assassinated in 1841, shortly before the British forces were driven out of Kabul and destroyed at the end of the First Anglo-Afghan War (1839–42), travelled widely in central Asia in the 1830s. He took with him texts of the Alexander historians, and went in search of the sites they mentioned. But he also noted that in parts of the region Alexander was considered an Islamic prophet, and mentions in his memoirs the (unprompted) claim of a local ruler to be a direct descendant of Alexander. These ideas of Alexander would probably have come through the *Romance* tradition as transmitted in Persian texts.

## Hero or villain

Perhaps the most influential study of Alexander to emerge from this period was that of the German historian Johann Gustav Droysen, whose *Geschichte Alexanders des Grossen* (*History of*

*Alexander the Great*—a work never translated into English) was published in 1833. Droysen studied in Berlin, and was influenced by the philosopher Hegel and the geographer Alexander von Humboldt. Enlightenment scholars in Germany identified their country closely with ancient Greece, not least because both were made up of a large number of small states surrounded by larger kingdoms. Droysen supported the cause of German unification, and his Alexander was also a unifier, not only of the warring Greek city-states, but of the whole of western Asia. For him the period that followed Alexander's death, until then seen as a time of decline in the Greek world, was actually one of triumph, as Greek culture sprang up in the territories through which his army had passed. What is more, Droysen suggested, Alexander's welcoming of men from many cultures into his court encouraged them to think about what they shared, including the idea of a single god: and therefore, perhaps, he paved the way for Christianity.

Alexander's contribution to civilization was depicted less positively by George Grote, a friend of the political philosopher John Stuart Mill and a radical MP, in his very popular 12-volume *History of Greece*. For Grote, Alexander represented all that was worst about autocracy and imperialism:

> As far as we can venture to anticipate what would have been Alexander's future, we can see nothing in prospect except years of ever-repeated aggression and conquest, not to be concluded until he had traversed and subjugated all the inhabited globe…Now, how such an empire thus boundless and heterogeneous, such as no prince has ever realized, could be administered with any advantage to subjects—it would be difficult to show.

The terms of the modern debate about Alexander were set in the Enlightenment. Historians still try to decide whether he was a romantic hero or a bloodthirsty tyrant, and whether or not his campaigns brought more good than harm. This is because, to a great extent, the arguments are based on the same limited collection of texts—the Alexander historians we considered at the start of this chapter. It is not my intention, at the end of this *Very Short Introduction*, to offer my own judgement on Alexander or his legacy. The surviving narratives can be interpreted to support a variety of assessments. It has been my aim, however, to show that these narratives are not necessarily reliable enough for us to use them to draw any clear conclusion at all. Material from Alexander's own time, in the form of the Greek and Egyptian inscriptions, the speeches of Athenian politicians, and the diaries of Babylonian scholar-priests, as we have seen, can offer some limited alternative perspective. Before asking, 'What should we think of Alexander the Great?', we should perhaps ask, 'What did his contemporaries think of Alexander the Great?'. That question has not yet been convincingly answered, but this book has been a start in that direction.

# References

## Introduction

Ada Cohen, *The Alexander Mosaic: Stories of Victory and Defeat* (Cambridge University Press, 1997)

Andrew Stewart, *Faces of Power: Alexander's Image and Hellenistic Politics* (University of California Press, 1993)

## Chapter 1: Before Alexander

Pierre Briant, *From Cyrus to Alexander: A History of the Persian Empire* (Eisenbrauns, 2002)

Lindsay Allen, *The Persian Empire* (British Museum Press, 2005)

Amélie Kuhrt, *The Persian Empire: A Corpus of Sources from the Achaemenid Period* (Routledge, 2007)

Robin Lane Fox (ed.), *Brill's Companion to Ancient Macedon: Studies in the Archaeology and History of Macedon, 650 BC–300 AD* (E.J. Brill, 2011)

## Chapter 2: Prince: Alexander in the Macedonian court

Elizabeth Carney, *Women and Monarchy in Macedonia* (University of Oklahoma Press, 2000)

Robin Lane Fox (ed.), *Brill's Companion to Ancient Macedon: Studies in the Archaeology and History of Macedon, 650 BC–300 AD* (E.J. Brill, 2011)

## Chapter 3: Warrior: Alexander's army

Donald W. Engels, *Alexander the Great and the Logistics of the Macedonian Army* (University of California Press, 1978)

Waldemar Heckel, *The Marshals of Alexander's Empire* (Routledge, 1992)

## Chapter 4:  Commander: Alexander and the Greeks

A.J. Heisserer, *Alexander the Great and the Greeks: The Epigraphic Evidence* (University of Oklahoma Press, 1980)

P.J. Rhodes and R.G. Osborne, *Greek Historical Inscriptions, 404–323 BC* (Oxford University Press, 2004)

## Chapter 5:  Pharaoh: Alexander and Egypt

Philip Bosman (ed.), *Alexander in Africa* (University of South Africa Press, 2014)

## Chapter 6:  King of the world: Alexander and Persia

Ernst Fredricksmeyer, 'Alexander the Great and the Kingship of Asia' in A.B. Bosworth and Elizabeth Baynham (eds), *Alexander the Great in Fact and Fiction* (Oxford University Press, 2000): 136–66

Hugh Bowden, 'On Kissing and Making Up: Court Protocol and Historiography in Alexander the Great's "Experiment with *Proskynesis*"', *Bulletin of the Institute of Classical Studies* 56/2 (2013): 55–77

Klaus Mann, *Alexander: A Novel of Utopia* (Brewer and Warren, 1930)

Mary Renault, *The Persian Boy* (Longman, 1972)

## Chapter 7:  Traveller: Alexander in Afghanistan and Pakistan

Joseph Naveh and Shaul Shaked, *Aramaic Documents from Ancient Bactria from the Khalili Collections* (Khalili Collections, 2012)

Frank Holt, *Into the Land of Bones: Alexander the Great in Afghanistan* (Second edn, University of California Press, 2012)

Steven Pressfield, *The Afghan Campaign* (Doubleday, 2006)

A.B. Bosworth, *Alexander and the East: The Tragedy of Triumph* (Oxford University Press, 1998)

## Chapter 8:  Doomed to die: Alexander in Babylon

Amélie Kuhrt, 'Alexander and Babylon', *Achaemenid History* 5 (1990): 121–30

R.J. van der Speck, 'Darius III, Alexander the Great and Babylonian Scholarship', *Achaemenid History* 13 (2003): 289–346

## Chapter 9:  After Alexander

Diana Spencer, *The Roman Alexander: Reading a Cultural Myth* (University of Exeter Press, 2002)

Richard Stoneman, *Alexander: A Life in Legend* (Yale University Press, 2008)

Claude Mossé, *Alexander: Destiny and Myth* (Johns Hopkins University Press, 2004)

C.A. Hagerman, *Britain's Imperial Muse: The Classics, Imperialism, and the Indian Empire, 1784–1914* (Palgrave Macmillan, 2013)

# Further reading

**Ancient narrative sources**

All modern reconstructions of the narrative of Alexander's life have to start with the ancient accounts, which are available in translation.

Arrian, *The Campaigns of Alexander*, translated by Aubrey de Sélincourt (Penguin Classics, 1958; revised edn 1971)

Arrian, *Alexander the Great: The Anabasis and the Indica*, translated by Martin Hammond (Oxford World's Classics, 2013)

Arrian, *The Landmark Arrian: The Campaigns of Alexander*, translated by Pamela Mensch (Anchor Books, 2012)

Plutarch, *The Age of Alexander*, translated by Ian Scott-Kilvert, revised by Timothy Duff (Penguin Classics, 1973; revised edn 2012)

Plutarch, *Greek Lives*, translated by Robin Waterfield (Oxford World's Classics, 2008)

Quintus Curtius Rufus, *The History of Alexander*, translated by John Yardley (Penguin Classics, 1984)

Diodorus Siculus, *Books 16.66–17*, translated by C. Bradford Welles (Loeb Classical Library, 1963)

Justin, *Epitome of the Philippic History of Pompeius Trogus*. Volume I Books 11–12: *Alexander the Great*, translated by John Yardley (Oxford University Press, 1994)

Waldemar Heckel and John Yardley, *Alexander the Great: Historical Sources in Translation* (Wiley-Blackwell, 2004) contains a wide selection of texts from more fragmentary sources.

## Modern biographies of Alexander

Biographies of Alexander the Great continue to be published at a rapid rate. Two that have stood the test of time are:

Robin Lane Fox, *Alexander the Great* (Allen Lane, 1973)

A.B. Bosworth, *Conquest and Empire* (Cambridge University Press, 1988)

A useful reference work is:

Waldemar Heckel. *Who's Who in the Age of Alexander the Great* (Wiley, 2006)

Something of the landscape through which Alexander travelled can be seen in:

Michael Wood, *In the Footsteps of Alexander the Great* (BBC DVD, 1998)

# Index

# HERODOTUS
## A Very Short Introduction
Jennifer T. Roberts

*Herodotus: A Very Short Introduction* introduces readers to what little is known of Herodotus' life and goes on to discuss all aspects of his work, including his fascination with his origins; his travels; his view of the world in relation to boundaries and their transgressions; and his interest in seeing the world and learning about non-Greek civilizations. We also explore the recurring themes of his work, his beliefs in dreams, oracles, and omens, the prominence of women in his work, and his account of the battles of the Persian Wars.

www.oup.com/vsi

# SOCIAL MEDIA
# Very Short Introduction

# Join our community
www.oup.com/vsi

- Join us online at the official Very Short Introductions **Facebook** page.
- Access the thoughts and musings of our authors with our online **blog**.
- Sign up for our monthly **e-newsletter** to receive information on all new titles publishing that month.
- Browse the full range of Very Short Introductions online.
- Read **extracts** from the Introductions for free.
- Visit our library of **Reading Guides**. These guides, written by our expert authors will help you to question again, why you think what you think.
- If you are a teacher or lecturer you can order inspection copies quickly and simply via our website.